T0381136

Orphan

LYNN ERNESTINE

◇~~~~~~ Copyrights: Etc.~~~~~~◇

WestBow Press books may be ordered through booksellers or by contacting:

WestBow Press
A Division of Thomas Nelson & Zondervan
1663 Liberty Drive
Bloomington, IN 47403
www.westbowpress.com
844-714-3454

ISBN: 979-8-3850-1094-3 (sc)
ISBN: 979-8-3850-1095-0 (e)

Library of Congress Control Number: 2023920649

Print information available on the last page.

WestBow Press rev. date: 12/6/2024

WESTBOW
PRESS®
A DIVISION OF THOMAS NELSON
& ZONDERVAN

◇◇◇◇◇◇◇◇~~~~~~ Contents ~~~~~~◇◇◇◇◇◇◇

◇◇◇◇◇◇~~Appreciation~~~◇◇◇◇◇◇

With gratitude to my family for accepting this time-consuming

endeavor. I have been making attempts to write a book for many years.

With their patience and support, now it is done.

With gratitude to my friends for their assistance, knowledge,

encouragement, and guidance, now it is done.

Our writing groups, "Right Writers" and "WOWW," have been the source of needed wisdom, guidance, and critiquing.   Special thanks go to Annette Byrd, Rosina Armon, and Dorothy Fleshman for their constant encouragement and help.

Good writing is **like an apple**

With **its surface** polished to perfection,

With **its flesh** the sweet taste of knowledge,

With **its core** the true value which produces

With **its seeds** of new understanding.

(May you gain **new understanding** from this story.)

To My Readers

In this book, you may notice capital letters on those names of animals which are frequent visitors at the Five-Acre Farm. That is because they visit like friends as they wander across fields, approach from behind bushes, sleep near the buildings, sing in the trees, feed from gifted food, etc. Their names are honored with capital letters because they become like friends. I also give them words for more interesting "dialogue." Please forgive these written faux pas and simply enjoy the animals in our world.   **Happy Reading, Lynn**

<>◇<>~~~~~~~~~ **Preface** ~~~~~~~~~~<>◇<>

Grandma and Grandpa are the characters in this story. She is also the author and Grandpa is in her story as he is in her life. She shares their story, as honestly as she can recall it, about a special time in their lives. As they aged, their love for the earth and its animals increased. They were richly blessed by their home, which sat between the mountains and the town. There they saw animal emotions: joy, love, grief, need, selfishness, fear, and many more human-like emotions. This elderly couple saw animals **"with their hearts, as well as with their eyes."**

Understanding and love develops between humans and animals. Body language is interpreted almost like words spoken and understood. Then hearts break when for some reason there is a separation. This author knows that kind of heartbreak because "much-loved "pets have short lives.

Wildlife is considered as different than pets, simply because it is less often experienced. This author was a teacher who strived to give her students experiences with animals. She purchased sea-horses, hermit crabs, tropical fish, and goldfish. She welcomed pollywogs, hatched blow flies, and had a terrarium containing a salamander pair. Students fed earthworms to the salamanders and even discovered the pair was smart. When a student approached, the salamanders knew to rush toward the glass and look upward hoping for a worm.

One of this teacher's most precious memories is when a Monarch butterfly was hatched and flew around the room often landing on young human bodies or even on tough little boy cheeks. One boy stood very still smiling and enjoying that cheek experience. After a few days the whole class merrily chased across the field following when the butterfly was released and flew away. Those children were seeing with their hearts as well as with their eyes. (Funny thing is that the butterfly returned to rest, outside of their classroom window where it landed and stayed for a while. It had circled in flight to come back.)

Grandma had hoped to develop, in her students, appreciation and knowledge about animals. The students did enjoy experiencing those animals and they learned some about them.

Few humans really understand wild animals unless they spend quality time observing them. Grandma and Grandpa had a wonderful opportunity to experience many kinds of wildlife and learned just as the children did. This story is about that wildlife and knowledge gained about those animals which had visited their farm. The author hopes this story can help the reader understand how special all animals are and how much like us they are. May you, the reader,
see animals **"with your hearts, as well as with your eyes."**

><><><>~~~~Excerpts of Poetry~~~~<><><

By William Wordsworth

(From <u>I Wandered Lonely as a Cloud</u>)

I wandered lonely as a cloud

That floats on high o'er vales and hills,

When all at once I saw a crowd,

A host, of golden daffodils

Beside the lake, beneath the trees,

Fluttering and dancing in the breeze.

By Lynn Ernestine

<u>I Wandered Lonely as a Child</u>

I wandered lonely as a child

With friends away and clouds of gray.

When all at once with thoughts of "wild,"

A Robins chirp gave news about the day.

The air was sweet, a cooling breeze,

The Earth summoned, dropped to my knees.

Beyond the rise, "wild" met my eyes.

New friends abound, they are all around.

Awesome view, I cannot rise.

Deer resting silent in the trees, were found.

No longer lonely midst' the "wild."

No longer now… a lonely child.

Chp. 1: "Predator and Prey"

With green eyes fixed and tail slightly twitching the cougar waited for exactly the right moment. Early sunrise allowed the cougar to pick its choice from the little herd of Mule Deer which was just rousing in the meadow. The patient cat had crept close enough so probability was great it would have its warm breakfast—soon, very soon!

About then one old doe caught the cougar's scent, jerked her head with eyes in its direction, and coughed a loud warning to the other deer. Instantly all were up and racing for their lives in random directions.

Cougar made its choice, and quick as a sprung trap, it was after a young one. Big paws covered the ground with huge leaps. Its strong muscles propelled it forward, like huge coiled springs releasing energy with quick bursts.

A deer with a good lead might have a chance to outrun such a predator. Although the fawn had practiced racing for just such a chase, the little one knew it was in trouble. ***Behind me—fast! Danger! Danger -danger is great – others feared – go, legs, go****! As the fawn raced it looked for a place to escape the pursuer, so it sped beside the gully toward the barn and fruit trees. Its small-boned legs and tiny hard hooves also seemed charged with springs as it moved in long low bounds, bouncing back up instantly when its toes touched upon the snow.

Up legs up! Over the first fence it leaped and turned to jump the deep gully which had been cut yearly by rushing water from the hill above. Then after crossing the deep channel, the fawn would have to jump another wire fence at the gully's edge. But that was an unwise plan. Snow had made it impossible to jump the next fence. ***Must go another way****!

Cougar was nearly on the fawn, so it spun toward the barn and shelter of a thorn bush. That, too, was an unwise action because then it was trapped at its front by a wooden fence and between the wooden wall of the loafing shed and a thick bush. Nothing was there behind it to stop the cougar's attack. Young deer died there under the thorny bush and that cougar had a fresh meal!

That cougar kill had occurred a few days before Grandma and Grandpa Mitchell returned from a trip to see their daughter's family with her new baby. The old couple were "travel frazzled" because they had crossed the borders of five states to see that baby. The baby was named Taylor, a name from Grandma's family. It was the first baby to give them the names "Grandma and Grandpa."

Quickly, after returning home, the old couple set about getting their house warmed and all things back in order. Then, with luggage inside and fire snapping and crackling from their wood stove, they looked toward the outside property.

"Wonder why all those birds are hanging around the bushes and barn?" Grandma asked when she saw Magpies noisily arguing about something, while other birds added to the commotion.

"Yeah, it looks like they might be scavenging on something dead," Grandpa observed.

"Well, what could it be?' Grandma questioned, but of course Grandpa would not know yet, so she headed to the barn to find out for herself. The bushes behind the barn were just a large thick growth of Buckbrush which had long thorns and fall berries. When Grandma and Grandpa established their home on the five-acre piece of land, they did not destroy the several brushy areas naturally there and the large apple tree which was also planted by nature beside the spring. The elderly couple wanted nature to prevail where verdant growth made good food and shelter for both domestic and wild animals.

Behind the barn also was a fun place for Grandma and Grandpa's children to build forts, tree houses, and all sorts of hideouts in that close little wild haven. The big old apple tree (old even when they made their home on the acreage) was just a "seedling" which meant it produced low quality apples. However, animals loved its fruit. Strangely the apples ripened, then dropped slowly from the tree serving a daily wildlife feast which lasted long into winter.

Deer even slept in the corral where many apples landed. It was their own special "Garden of Eden," but it was the fence of this corral which had stopped the little deer. The young one had headed for what it thought would be safety, but then it could not get inside the corral.

Grandma saw the young deer's bloody body and sadness filled her. "T'was just a fawn," she said aloud, "Last year's baby…and that looks like a cougar kill!" She cautiously backtracked and carefully studied the big paw-prints and small hoof-prints, which were probably made a few days before, judging by how the snow had melted making the impressions larger. Since the prints were traveling the same path, she assumed the big cat was following the small deer. The failed jump across the gully showed clearly in the crushed muddy snow and then the hoof-prints changed direction. At that point there were no paw-prints, revealing that the cat must have leaped onto the little deer to bring it down.

"Poor little thing! Luck wasn't with it!" Cautiously Grandma scanned the bushes and fields to make sure the predator was not still lurking. She saw nothing unusual, but she remained nervous anyway. "God, no more carnivores, please," she mumbled and continued scanning the bushes and nearby fields to be safe.

She knew cougars often return to their kill and that meant one could be nearby. She remained watchful because she had no weapon to protect herself. When she looked closely at the dead fawn, she noticed injuries around its head and neck area. "This coulda' been your Momma killed 'stead of you. Might'a been worse for you that way. Life is hard for an orphan!"

Shaking her head, Grandma wiped away a few tears that were creeping down her cheeks and turned toward the house to tell Grandpa why the scavenging birds were flying overhead.

Grandma grieved even though this was a normal act of nature, but happening behind their barn made it too real. Grandpa had to get rid of the carcass quickly so the cougar would not return to its kill.

Grandpa mumbled to himself as he lifted the stiff little body into the back of his pickup, "Jus' too many predators! People in control don't know nothin'! If they did this wouldn't have happened!" Though he knew moving the little deer could cause legal complications for him, he loaded it and took it further into the mountains. In the mountains Mother Nature would finish her job and various wild creatures would be fed for a time. By man's law Grandpa was doing an illegal thing in transporting any deer anywhere, but by nature's logic that was the only thing he could do. He had to be sure humans or domestic animals would not meet that cougar near the barn. This was just common sense!

Their son, after he was grown, revealed his cougar experience when he was a teen. (Only told as an adult because otherwise his mother would have kept him too close.) The experience involved a cougar not far from their home. It happened when he and a friend walked on the railroad tracks which followed the nearby river on its course down the canyon. The boys often explored in this way as teenagers widening their horizons.

This one day they were bird hunters armed with shotguns. They heard only the chuckle of the water as they quietly walked down the tracks during grouse season. Their eyes were widely scanning for the wily little gray bird when suddenly a cougar blurred over their heads as it leaped from the bank above them. It had spotted a crow they had not seen perched on a limb in front of them. In the cougar's overhead jump it grabbed for the crow, but the crow flew away and the cougar landed in front of the boys as startled as they were. Neither had known the other was there, until suddenly they were face to face. Both boys and the cougar were studying their danger. What could happen to them?

There seemed little time for the boys to think as they stood with eyes wide and minds filled with panic. "Don't run!" one teen commanded as they both readied their shotguns.

The cougar had careened to the ground about forty feet in front of the shocked boys. Big cat switched ends to face them and began twitching its tail while crouching low and creeping toward them. Their guns were quickly lifted to their shoulders, shells loaded, and safety levers off. They each solidly placed their feet, braced their guns against their shoulders, then took a deep breath to be able to hold steady for a stable shot if the cougar kept coming or made an aggressive attack. They knew people must appear very large when near cougars, so the boys could not drop to their knees to shoot. On their knees they would look small.to the cougar.

The cat, with curled lips and fangs bared, kept snarling angrily. Was it a low rumble or a hiss? Either way it was a threat! In a slight crouch with its green eyes calculating and its tail nervously quivering back and forth, it kept slowly edging toward the boys stalking them. **Stalking them!** *Will we have to shoot?*

About then, **"Bang!"** one boy fired a blast of shot over the cougar's head. Then **"Shush! ... Thunk!"** The empty shell ejected and hopefully another chambered, but the cat just continued threatening by snarling and creeping forward as if the loud noises meant nothing to it. They knew the next shot would have to be dead center at a close target, because one distant pattern of shotgun pellets might not stop this angry predator. *There won't be time for two trigger pulls...maybe there's no shell in the other gun.* The boys' thoughts raced, but they just waited motionless.

"Oh, Daaaam!" one boy uttered as they stood in frozen readiness with their sights lined up, just waiting for the cougar to make its move.

After a tense face-off, with green eyes angry from its failure to get food, the angry cougar turned and clawed up over the bank. Its large paws and rippling leg muscles lunged it away and down toward the river. The cougar was still hungry, but it was too wise to attack guns. The questions loom, "What if they **had not** held guns? What if they **had** run in fear?"

There were no cougars seen at Grandma and Grandpa's Five-Acre Farm, but many tales were told of cougar presence nearby. Their farm sat on the north edge of the valley with the hill beyond. On that hill was a rock wall known to have at least once held a cougar female and her cubs. It was said the female was killed and the cubs taken captive, but such acts are often hidden from the world, so Grandma cannot verify any of that. What she did know was that cougars had visited the Five-Acre Farm more than once.

There was one evening just at dusk, after the Mitchells' daughter and son were home from school, when a loud animal call was heard which was unlike anything heard before. Their daughter was jumping rope on the sidewalk at the back of the house while their big white dog was somewhere out front. Suddenly a loud unidentified squall sent them both running. She rushed into the house very afraid and only knowing that the sound had come from somewhere toward the front of the house, the side toward the hill.

Their pet was later found hiding in fear at the back of the house. The big dog wanted nothing to do with the creature which made that sound. She may have even seen it before running to hide. After they found her, the gentle pet was hard to pull from her hiding place.

The questions about that creature which sounded so close to the house was never answered. However, most large predators are not noisy, but cougars can be. (Think about how noisy domesticated cats can be! A cougar is just a big wild cat.)

It might be a clue that the rock wall cliff north of the house, which has caves in it, can be seen across the road and field in front of the house...and cougars do hide in caves! Proof of that was the female with her babies found in the ice caves there.

The cougar kept creeping toward the boys.

STALKING THEM!

Chp. 2: "The World of Fawns"

Cougars had even been seen in the nearby town. At one home paw-prints had been often seen in a yard there on a routine basis. In months with snow on the ground those prints clearly showed and would not be confused with prints of any other animal. Perhaps cougars were just traveling to the other side of the valley, or maybe local deer might have been their attraction.

A little doe had repeatedly taken shelter on the patio of another home across the valley. It was not a matter of her seeking shelter from the weather. The family there could tell it was a matter of fear. They said the deer was there often and it appeared the little doe came to get away from a predator. Maybe it was escaping from a cougar or even wolves on the forested hillside behind their home. Both kinds of those predators had been seen there.

At the Mitchells' Farm there was once a set of big animal paw imprints seen in snow in the same place as deer hoof-prints. Both sets of tracks were made entering the Farm's north field through the front gate and both sets went to the corral. Grandma believed a cougar had followed a deer down to the corral. Grandpa argued, "Those were from that big white dog 'at wanders 'round the neighborhood! You know …Rod's dog!" Grandpa would not want Grandma to know cougars were near, even if he believed it himself, but she understood his thinking.

With a sigh and irritation, she responded, "No! Too long between the tracks! Cougars jump long!" It was a subject the old couple vehemently debated because similar tracks had been seen before in that field.

Their Farm was on the edge of the valley with town south of them and the hill to the north. Farther north were many rugged mountains, some so high they gave a view of three states at once. On that first hill was that rock wall with an ice cave known to have held the female cougar and her kittens. That same rock wall was seen from the Mitchell's front windows, though the cougar cave was out of sight. Logically young cougars would migrate from more remote mountains to the valleys below, where food was more available and where dominant adult cougars might not be competitors for hunting territories.

Many deer had taken up residence in the nearby town, probably to avoid predators, though cougars did pass through that town. Smart deer would live there because those neighborhoods held an abundance of edible plants and gardens. When living among people, deer could not be shot so they became fearless and even dined in yards and gardens which irritated many of the town citizens.

Fast-moving vehicles were the biggest danger to town deer. However, many deer remained at the fringes of town where wildlife rarely needed to dine on yards and gardens. Fruit trees did attract them and Grandma and Grandpa's land had several fruit trees, mostly apples and one prune tree.

The deer at the Mitchells' home got only forage and fruit because there were only apple and prune trees and a few strawberry plants. Even the fawns made their way into the yard to feast on prunes which fell onto the backyard lawn from the old petite tree.

Grandpa, as the father of a young family, had worked very diligently establishing their home. He moved posts, cement, and tools to all the outer fence lines by dragging them to where he installed a four-wire barbed fence. That was the first ever to encircle that property. A well was drilled and he plumbed in the water. A sewer system was put into virgin ground. Electricity was wired from the main lines on the road to the house. His choice of location had a view more beautiful than most with mountains and forests framing it. Even the evening chirping of crickets and croaking songs of frogs made the location especially desirable when choosing a location for the Mitchell home.

*Grandpa had built the corral, barn and other outbuildings nea*r the big old apple tree which later served for their son to climb and build his tree house. He and his sister in their young years enjoyed nature's places for their imagination games. The visits of nature on this Five-Acre Farm were probably as important to the family as the manufactured house the Mitchells placed down a lane from the road. During their first winter there, coyotes yodeled nearby, owls hooted from the nearest trees, and other wildlife remained very close, with deer even sleeping on the dirt hump that would become the family's back yard.

When the old couple's children were young, the family farm had boasted two gardens and various animals: one dog, two cats, calves, pigs, chickens, turkeys, horses, and a duck which had waddled alone up the road and into the driveway quacking as it came. Perhaps it just needed a home and it was welcomed. In later years those animals were all gone, leaving only one dog and one cat, a miniature American Eskimo and a resident stray calico puss. There was not even one small garden. A few stray animals still showed up now and then, but only wildlife seemed to claim the farm and that satisfied the elderly couple whose bodies were beginning to struggle with outdoor work.

After their five acres was no longer a productive farm, deer visited and ate fruit there. The old petite prune tree had been brought as a seedling from Grandpa's childhood home to be planted in the farm's backyard. It became an attraction in the fall for much wildlife. A woven chain-link fence, which surrounded the yard, was not an obstruction to adult deer as they leaped over to get to the prunes and anything else they desired. But it was impossible for fawns to cross to get inside. Until fawns grew old enough to make high jumps they sometimes panicked, racing from edge to edge fearing they would be left after the adults vaulted over fences and wandered away. Finally, the babies would find the hole through which they had entered, or another hole, or Grandma would sneak out unseen and open the side gate for them.

Deer would mostly disappear during hunting season, but after that passed, wildlife eventually returned to the valley. Then deer became almost routine visitors in Grandma and Grandpa's lives. Also, this was time or apples to be ripe. Some groups of deer would visit and then stay a while. Others would speedily pass through.

Sometimes it was Mule Deer, like the one killed by the cougar, but more rarely it was White Tails. The latter were far more skittish and never seemed to settle in one place. When a human appeared, they would raise their long white tails straight upward and flair the hair to make their tails appear large and highly visible. In this way they raced away from what they perceived as danger. White Tails were never friendly guests.

Perhaps a moving tail was planned by Mother Nature as a difficult target. It could have been planned to distract those trying to hurt them from seeing more vulnerable body parts. Maybe it was just to warn other White Tails to flee from danger. Humans can only guess! It is said that White Tails do not join with Mule Deer herds, but fawns must not yet know to "discriminate."

One day a Mule Deer fawn turned to see a herd of White Tail deer passing through the field in front of the barn. Then the cutest thing happened! One fawn from each group faced each other, walked cautiously together, curiously sniffed the other's nose, then after a short pause turned and walked away. Just not interested in a relationship! At least that is how it appeared, but there was no animosity or excitement shown. They just parted in peace with curiosity satisfied. The two herds did not really mingle. Instead, they just separated after the White Tails ate what they wanted and then quickly exited out the other side of the field, as if saying, ***"Just passing through, and have a good day."***

A different day Grandma saw two white "flags" bouncing one-after-the-other through tall heavily grown weeds in the neighbor's field. "Look over there in that next field," she urged Grandpa, while excitedly pointing, but his enthusiasm was never as great as hers. Little white objects were bouncing, high above the weeds and waving side-to-side rhythmically like a "downside-up" clock pendulum, as they sped around and around through the heavy growth. Grandma knew that beneath those "flags" were two baby White Tail deer playing tag. The pace of their little legs set the pace of their tail flop.

Right, left! Tick-tock! Tail flop! Go, feet, go! You can't catch me! Gotcha'…Now you chase me!

Then the circle of travel would go in the opposite direction with happy little legs racing just as fast as they could move through those weeds. Grandma imagined she could hear their childish giggles, like those of her now-grown son and daughter in similar games of chase during their long-ago childhood years.

Those baby deer really knew how to maneuver on their "stilty little legs." Corners were taken so sharp their white tails leaned into the turn like a rider on a fast-cornered motorcycle.

Fawn play must have been designed as practice for a time when agility might save them from a predator, but it was only for fun on this day—a friendly race and playing tag. The fawn action was very much like children at play, happy children racing and playing tag. It should be noted here that the "children" had mothers standing by to make sure their little ones were safe.

Many nimble limbs were finding movement fun in their play which continued until nervous mamas took the babies back to their birth bushes for the night. Mamas had learned Mother Nature provides two extremes: joy like fawn play, or suffering such as that of the little fawn found behind the barn. All watchful mamas have many responsibilities.

Not all baby deer survive those very first days. Grandpa and Grandma knew that fact because they happened upon a scene in which a fawn was killed; its mama could do nothing to keep that from occurring. As the Mitchells and a couple of friends were driving in the mountains, they came upon a skittish little doe darting back and forth near the road. While wondering what was causing her behavior, the travelers inside the car watched and slowly progressed on down the road.

Then they saw a big cinnamon-colored female bear quickly sniffing while looking at the ground near the road as if searching for something. Logic said she was hunting for the doe's baby. Coming behind the sow bear were two little brown cubs, following until she sent them scurrying up a large pine tree where they waited and watched. It was just seconds before the sow's demeaner showed she could smell something. Then she rushed directly to a huge embedded rock with its height serving as a hiding place for the baby deer. With one quick lunge the sow grabbed the fawn's whole body in her mouth then shook it violently. Little legs protruded from her mouth, making it obvious the fawn would not survive. Humans cringed but nothing could be done to stop that action.

After the bear dropped the fawn, she did not eat from it, but instead went to her cubs and called them down to feast on the "fresh meat." They ate willingly as if this was not a new experience. The twins ripped at the little body while mother bear stood back. She even stood on her hind legs so she could see and threaten anything which might be approaching. Probably her stance was also meant to look huge and ferocious, and it did!

Humans in the car knew they had seen nature's best and worst all at one time. Their hearts hurt for the pain experienced in this, and they knew it was an event which probably occurred often in the wild. The car with its occupants left but, after their short trip down the road and back, they passed the site again. Mama bear was still standing there on her hind legs guarding while the cubs feasted, and the little doe was still in the distance fidgeting while trying to see her baby. It was obvious the little doe was trying to get as close as she could to her baby, but she was afraid.

"Nature's best" was the mother love demonstrated by the mother bear and the mother deer. "Nature's worst" was that it involved the killing act to provide food for the little bear cubs. Another worst" was the suffering of the mother deer who was not able to protect her baby.

The little doe also had humans to fear, those who were driving very close to where she left her baby, but the bear was her greatest fear. She knew her baby was being hunted by the bear, but she also knew there was nothing she could do about that. Her own life was also in danger as she peered around bushes and trees to see what was happening. She was afraid! Very afraid!

The little doe had love for her baby, just like humans love their babies. She did not yet know that her baby no longer lived. She surely did know that a bear was a very dangerous animal which could show up at any time in the places where she lived; that was obvious in her actions. Many wild ones must always be watching to avoid attacks, unless they are at the top of the food chain.

"Time for Milk"
September 15, 2013 at 3:56 A.M.
(Taken with a trail camera.)

**Some hunting seasons start in early September.
Does this fawn look ready to lose its mother?**

Chp. 3: "Windows into the Wild World"

A veritable love grew between the older lonesome couple and the wildlife which visited their small piece of land, their "Five-Acre Farm" as Grandma always called it. Wildlife became her friends seen mostly through her windows.

Grandma even watched one courtship between a three-point buck and a young twinkle-eyed doe who was obviously fascinated by his majesty. The beautiful buck was so enamored he pursued and posed for the doe outside Grandma's kitchen window as if unaware of human presence. Deer actions convinced Grandma they are more like humans than we even imagine. She could almost hear spoken words from the "twitterpated" couple ("Twitterpated" is a word from the "Bambi" book.) This deer love affair will be shared in detail after they gain identities later in this book.

Grandma enjoyed watching several Mule Deer as they moved close and showed no fear. They came to the farm almost daily in fall when apples were ripe and dropping. Grandma would sit outside on the deck singing and plunking on her father's old banjo and the deer would pass near the yard fence, even nibbling grass which grew just outside the fence wires. They were not bothered by human music – maybe even liked it. "You are my sunshine…" often filled the air, possibly off pitch but the deer did not seem to mind.

Deer visits revealed their graceful beauty, watchful presence, social interactions, seasonal changes, mating rituals, relationship with all of nature, and even their human-like mother and child affection. Watching deer struggle for survival during their seasonal challenges brought interest into Grandma and Grandpa's lives. She observed actions regarding these wild behaviors as she watched from the house windows. She could almost feel the warmth as she observed a doe licking her fawn's face and body, while the fawn was absolutely soaking up the attention.

"Guess we should make them fear us," Grandma often said to Grandpa, but they just could not do the hazing required to make deer stay away. Deer appeared to consider the Mitchell house just a part of their world and not a threat. In fact, one set of little orphans even snuggled down outside the yard gate which Grandma had just walked through. She had seen them coming up from the bottom bushes, so before they arrived, she rushed to the old apple tree with a rake to knock out apples for them. Perhaps they knew she gave them food or maybe they felt Grandma's love while she then watched from inside the house windows.

After eating apples, the little buck settled with his back resting against that same gate and his sister followed there. He seemed to be the leader, but she sniffed around and finally rested next to him. Both had their tummies full and warm sunshine on their bodies. No other deer were near them, but they seemed happy just to have a human nearby, especially one who had fed them apples.

Another special time the orchard garden held orphan twins. They were there to escape persistent rain while snuggled together underneath the heavily laden apple branches. Perhaps it was the same little pair who had shared the gate. Together the little pair found shelter, companionship, comfort, and food all in one location. They must have felt safe in that small abandoned garden because it was a wire-fenced enclosure with its gate always open. Also, it had the reassuring scent of many other deer who frequently spent time inside while gleaning apples or resting in its apple-tree shade.

Through the years there were several fawns orphaned because of game hunting rules, fast traffic, and gun-happy humans. Orphans had to survive in a world which did not want them and they had no parent to protect them. If possible, they stayed with their herd, but often they were fought from food by some in the herd using butting heads and pawing feet. The orphans were only allowed to sleep at a distance from all the others in the herd.

When deer stayed until after dark in the bottom field Grandma would sometimes shine a flashlight over the sleeping herd. She usually saw pairs of shiny eye reflections where deer were nestled close together, but often one set of eyes was seen spaced away from the others. The lone pair of eyes must have belonged to an orphan trying to stay as close to the herd as was allowed. Grandma reasoned. *If a predator was near the herd and belonged to those separate eyes, the herd would not have been resting calmly.* The fawn was not a threat, just unwelcome.

There were few exceptions to deer rejection of orphans. However, one doe from another herd once took care of four fawns, welcoming the extra two. Grandma was never able to verify if that doe allowed only her fawns to nurse. There were times when orphans found food and safety at the Five-Acre Farm when abandoned by their herd.

Sometimes orphans would travel with young single bucks who were also ostracized from the group, but that was difficult for fawns because young bucks were rapid travelers--like teenagers. The orphans were not actually welcomed by young bucks, but they were allowed "to hang-out together" until the buck suddenly raced away, leaving the fawns far behind.

One little injured orphan doe could even be called from the bushes to approach within four feet of Grandma where the little one then waited for tossed apples. Grandma's repeated words, "Si-i-i-is, …Come here, Sis," became a familiar sound for the little doe, demonstrated by her ears lifting and rotating forward, her eyes turning to the sound, and her feet starting to move her out of the bushes toward Grandma who was standing in the yard.

The apples given to the fawn had to be cut into smaller pieces because otherwise she choked. A bullet injury was logical to explain the fawn's choking. There was a dark spot on her neck which was eventually believed to be the entry hole for a bullet which had exited through another dark spot seen beneath her neck.

When first injured the little doe had stayed many days lying in the corral where she could watch the house. Without this safe place providing her shelter and protection, as well as access to water and food, she might have been another fatal victim of someone with a gun.

During winters, hostile weather pummeled the earth and all on it. Grandma and Grandpa Mitchell's wood stove radiated heat indoors, but outdoors they fought winter's battles. Icicles hung from the roof, sometimes even twenty-four inches long. The front sidewalk on the north side of the house often drifted full, and maybe up to the eaves, requiring hand shoveling. Grandpa plowed the long lane to the house with his little green two-cylinder "Poppin' Johnny" tractor which had cleated tracks to grab through thick slick snow. It was hard work just to be able to leave the farm. They never went south to warmer weather regardless of winter misery on their farm.

In the mountainous area, where the Five-Acre Farm sits, only those animals surviving winter had adapted to its extremes. They were the ones which have evolved to withstand cold and hunger, and evade hungry predators. Some animals simply hibernated or made body adaptations like thicker hair or fur coverings. All animals survived only if they had some means of resisting the painful cold and the knife sharp cut of wind and snow.

The deer even became a different color with their new longer heavier winter coats—a camouflage change as well as insulation. Deer can sleep blanketed by snow and probably not feel the cold, but extremes of weather causes death of even the hardiest animals when watering holes freeze and icy crusts of snow make finding food impossible. Winters in that corner of Oregon were difficult for all animals. They got a miserable beating by an angry Mother Nature. Outdoor cats for example often could not survive without human help. Against the white snow a highly colored cat became visible prey for the many winter-hungry predators.

Coyotes roamed and howled, even from nearby fields, though they knew they were being watched by humans. Large owls perched on the limbs of the yard's shade trees with watchful eyes. Hawks often circled in flight over the fields searching from above for their next dinner. Even the white heads of bald eagles were seen in flight and they could and would easily attack prey the size of a cat. Therefore, cats and other small animals needed a shelter in which to hide and stay warm.

On one "minus-fourteen degree" morning a neighbor's horse fell on the slick frozen pond below the Mitchells' house. The owner was at work, so she was called. Others heard about the need for help and several came with ropes and other devices to assist, but there was little success in getting the big animal upright. It thrashed and struggled to lift its body. Front up, rear down, feet slid and the horse repeatedly came crashing to the ice, sometimes hitting its head with a loud thud.

The thought of using something to roughen the ice, like sand, was impossible because everything outside was frozen solid. Garden soil, road sand, and sawdust were considered, but could not be loosened. Grandpa and others worked to finally roll the horse onto its side on the bank of the pond, but it still could not get to its feet.

Wild turkeys steal birdseed.

Grandma watched through binoculars from the house window as it rolled its eyes and died. Maybe the horse died because it repeatedly crashed to the ice, or was death caused by the extreme cold chilling its body which had become damp with struggle perspiration? If its owners had provided accessible drinking water, it would not have gone onto the ice to reach the unfrozen spot for a drink. Thirst made it die! Grandma was sad, but then she grew mad and vented her anger to Grandpa's ears, "Why don't people have a roof, water, and food for animals they trap behind fences? That animal had to go onto ice!" Grandma was angry!

Grandpa just nodded his head in agreement, then replied, "Yeah. You don't ever wanta' trust ice, or get wet out in the cold. It'll get you!"

Most wild birds fly to warmer climes, but not all. Turkeys which were transplanted as a new game bird from a warmer origin had multiplied, but they did suffer terribly in their new environment. This corner of Oregon is not the climate for which they had evolved. They match the description of Mexican wild turkeys.

At the farm on winter days, hungry wild turkeys trekked across frozen fields as a flock following the leader to find food. In their coldest low-energy part of the day they might stop to rest, but for nights they flew into their chosen tall pine tree up on the hill; perhaps they were a little warmer and safer there. Their leader was the tom, sometimes called a "cock" or "gobbler."

Fall was turkey time for returning to the valley. It has been said that the returning mass is called together and led by a noisy tom, a "Pied-Piper" in a parade toward the haven of the valley. ("Pied" means dressed in a garment of many colors and "colorful" does describe a Tom Turkey.) Flocks gathered in great numbers in the valley with each hen bringing her poults, her babies numbering sometimes around twenty. The valley was their hope of surviving the winter.

In spring the toms spread their tails like a fan and "strut their stuff" to impress and fertilize as many hens as possible. Young toms just stood back to avoid a fight; this is nature's way to reproduce only the mightiest. The big toms were an awesome sight, "almost other-worldly" with their bright red snood and wattle (skin dangling over and under their beak) and a gloss of bright metallic green, copper, and bronze on their feathers. Sunlight also created an iridescent blue and green reflection on the featherless red skin of turkey heads and necks. (Definitely a "Pied Piper").

After springtime mating, the flocks scattered into the hills separately so the hens could raise their broods undisturbed during summertime, eating nature's bugs, berries, grasses, seeds, etc. Grandma did not see any of their speckled tan eggs, but "Encyclopedia World Book" says the eggs are laid in "crude nests of dried leaves on the ground." Also, it says, "The male turkey often tries to break the hens' eggs, and because of that the hen turkeys find hiding places for their nests." *So that is the reason the turkeys scattered in the summer and one little lone hen often came to the Five-Acre Farm's watering hole,* Grandma understood. *The little hen was living alone to protect her babies.*

A highlight of Grandma's window watching was when little Cottontail rabbits showed up at the farm. They seemed unaffected by cold weather. Grandma knew facts about bunnies as told by others, "For snowy days of winter, they wear white coats, but spring makes them brown. It is nature's camouflage.

Their coats help hide them from winter predators since a white coat on white snow seems to disappear. A brown coat serves them well in other seasons because it blends so well with earth colors and natural growth, like bushes."

One sunny spring day Grandma was surprised to see a trio of bunnies bouncing through the field, across the yard, and into her flower bed. They were not the domesticated kind, but obviously wild ones. She thought they were probably what she knew as "Cotton Tails." She believed them to be smaller than others in the rabbit family and these three were small. It was a surprise to see the bouncy little ones at the farm. They seemed to be enjoying the yard as much as the expanse of the field.

The bunnies must have been young because they were very lively and quick. One of their games involved something like "automobile chicken." Two bunnies would have a "face-off" then "rev-up their motors" and head directly toward each other until one would spring about three feet straight up while spinning around in the air as the other raced beneath. By the time Jumping Bunny landed Running Bunny had flopped ends making them both ready for another attack.

Grandma could almost hear Jumping Bunny laughing, ***"Ha! Ha! You missed again!***

Then Running Bunny responding, ***"I'll get you yet, you Wotton Wabbit!"***

Finally, they chased through the buried drainpipe and dodged among dormant plants. They seemed to enjoy that drainpipe best. It must have resembled a typical rabbit hole in the ground because they would go in one open end of the pipe, scoot through it, and emerge later about ten feet from the entry.

Those little wild rabbits also seemed to enjoy the flowerbed which extended the length of the yard beside the front fence. At the time they were there, the flowers were dormant or gone but still provided obstacles for them to dodge over and around while bounding through a cover of snow.

They were having a great time bucking and kicking sideways, with bunny tails often flapping the air and little paddle feet cornering like a skier. Maybe bunny thoughts were, ***Life is so fun and I'm not worried about a thing! Beware of the Big Bad Wolf? Naaaaaa!***

In trying to remember what color they were, Grandma "drew a blank," but that may be because they were between shedding their brown coats to become white or vice-versa to become brown. There would be some stage in which they would be a blend for a while. Surely their change of color also meant a change in their warmth, so they would be better protected from the cold in wintertime and yet not too hot in summertime.

Grandma enjoyed their wonderful small show which even extended around the front field in a competitive race. It was large loops which they traveled in their race. Around and around! She hoped they would often visit again. Their happiness just seemed to spread happiness, sending Grandma to her work with a smile on her face.

However, bunnies were never seen again.

Chp.4: "Deer Lessons"

One Mule Deer doe was often seen at the farm. She was identifiable by her torn right ear. Perhaps the tear was from a bullet, a limb, or a barbed-wire fence. Since that doe was one which they could recognize Grandma said, "We'll call her Delawna." (As a child Grandma had read and reread a version of the book "Bambi" in which Bambi's mother was named Felawna. For this reason, Grandma changed just one letter and had the name for another sweet doe.)

Spring always brought relief for animals, a happy radiant earth, human comfort, and a rebirth of all living things. Deer bred in the fall gave birth to their babies, usually in May or June. Some fawns were birthed in nearby brush patches, and even in the section along the south fence of the Five-Acre Farm. That section was fenced on four sides and was rarely opened for grazing, so with its padding of old dried plants it became a protected nest for young animals. Delawna may have been born there herself a few years prior. She knew to find it when "her time came," and she did use that brush patch for her baby which was born in May. Does go into seclusion when they give birth. Only after their baby gains strength can they return to company of other deer.

Deer birth must be like that of cattle – first the baby's front hooves emerge on long legs and then out comes its head and body. Hopefully the doe is supine so the fawn does not have a hard landing. Then the doe would lick and swallow the protective membrane from its body. This cleans, dries, and opens baby's airway. Nothing of the bloody birthing process must remain as scent to attract predators. Surely that was what Delawna did. That first cleaning develops a love between doe and fawn while it gives the mother recognition of the scent of her one special baby. That scent of her baby becomes so impressed in the doe she could find her baby "in a crowd with just one whiff."

The fawn would be scent free such that a predator could walk nearby and not even know the fawn was there, especially after its mama taught it to drop to the ground and not move a muscle. A snort or nudge from the doe would send an obedient baby collapsing to the ground. Later its long legs help it flee, but, as a baby with wobbly legs, its protection is invisibility.

Grandma knows how motionless they lie because she and Grandpa once found one in the woods. They saw the doe "put it down" and then scurry away to entice predators to follow her. How motionless that baby laid, not even an eyelash moved. Grandma could not resist just touching the soft wavy scent-free baby hair. Gently, with only one finger, she dared only one touch because more might endanger it with human scent, possibly causing its mama to not return. Baby did not even flinch at human touch. The old couple drove on but looked back to see the doe returning to her fawn. No damage had been done.

Surely, that is what Delawna's baby would also do. Delawna stayed with her baby while nursing, protecting, licking, and sleeping with it. The fawn knew to stay there hidden in the "Bottom Bushes" while she wandered away for food. The doe was taking a break from the nursery. Every morning and evening she would sneak out to eat and refresh herself, doing so increasingly longer each day. She needed water, but her baby did not because it got liquid from nursing. Her daily leaving and returning were clues for Grandma and Grandpa about what she had hidden, so humans did not go there.

"Since it's Delawna's baby we'll call it Dawna and pretend it's a girl," Grandma suggested to Grandpa who did not argue the point. He thought her silly, though, because he believed determining deer gender was not possible until males got antlers. What they did not know was that little nubbins show up on the head very soon on male fawns…something Grandma later learned through her windows.

Another birth had occurred in an adjoining field in a different patch of brush. "Look there!" Grandma urged while pointing. "That other doe has been staying around, too. Guess we'll call her Mama Deer 'cause prob'ly she has a baby hidden in that neighbor's field. Wonder what it is…or…maybe twins?"

The brush patches were close together, so both does often found food while walking through the meadow together. Then eventually adventurous babies wandered after their mamas and met. That began their fun. Tiny legs frolicked in small circles around their mothers and then in larger circles. Around the field they played chase-and-dodge and anything else spindly legs could manage. Spring happiness was so sweet it required a deer dance, the dodge-and-dart, jump-and-spin, with ears low and corners sharp, with tails a-flying out behind. Even Delawna and Mama Deer had to join in as the babies played.

Go, feet, go! You can't catch me! …Ha! Ha! But what is this? Two more racers?

There really were two more babies which had joined the deer dance. They belonged to another doe, who was either passing through or who had birthed nearby. One fawn was smaller and appeared to always be the last at "the milk bar." The other was quite large, though the twin births must have been at the same time. Nature just does that sometimes. Anyway, the twins were both healthy and had lots of stamina for the chase.

When Grandma saw the twins, she decided they also needed names so they became Big-un and Little-un, the "children" of Twin Mama. It seemed Grandma just had to name everything. She told Grandpa, "A critter without a name is as bad as a pan without a handle…jus' somethin' ya' gotta fix." So then Twin Mama and the twins became as much a part of Grandma and Grandpa's life as the first two does and their fawns. Sometimes a very young buck would show up who acted as if he had been Twin Mama's fawn from the year before. He wanted to be close to her, but she did not want him to be near her. She would act angry and rush at him in ways that would make him stand back.

There were eight members to the little herd when they were all together. That number fluctuated because sometimes other deer joined them, but sometimes some also left.

As spring and summer progressed the does and their babies began to migrate more and mix with other deer. They were even seen in the barn brush patch with White Tails there also. The demeanor of all was that of inquisitiveness and hesitation – like strangers at a family party. They just studied each other and took hesitant steps. They seemed only to be distant cousins, not really like family.

One of the lessons Delawna and Mama Deer's babies learned was where to find good seeds, those called "deer candy." Grandpa would put bird seed on the ground for quail and in a high feeder for little birds. Delawna and Mama Deer often jumped the fence and nibbled right out of the high bird feeder in the yard, sometimes turning to look a little nervously into the house window but remaining undaunted at their theft. The young ones could only stick their noses and tongues through the fence wires to pick up seeds from the ground, because they still could not jump over the fence to get inside.

One day Grandma stood hidden behind the kitchen window watching the fawns stretch their tongues through the wire fence, she noticed little bumps on top of Mama Deer's baby's head. Right between his big flappy ears were two small nubbins about the size of black olives. They were the beginning of antlers, and so soon, but they were surely there and not on the other little fawn. So that meant Dawna really was a female! That meant Mama Deer's baby was a male!

Grandma smiled as she held an inside-the-house one-sided conversation with the little outside fawn, "You are a little buck! I guessed it because of how rough you play. Now I can give you a name. You are now called Little Buck, because it is certain you are one."

The fawns had much to learn in their young years. Their biggest lesson seemed to be "barbed-wire fences." Fawns were too little to jump over fences like their mothers easily did and, if a fence was tight, there might be no way to wiggle through it. They probably thought, ***Mom, everybody, wait! I can't get to you. Don't leave me!***

Frantic babies often ran up and down the wrong side of the fence while the herd nonchalantly moved on. *What to do? What to do?* Then wise fawns would find a high bottom wire they could wiggle under, or a hole from a broken wire, or a low top wire, or two widely separated wires they could wiggle between. All alternatives held danger and many fawns died or were injured in just such a predicament. Those unable to extricate themselves from the wire trap sometimes died there. Most dangerous was when they tried jumping over but did not quite make it, so the upper wires would wrap around their legs. Wise babies waited until they were big and strong to try that "over the top" jump.

Fawns learned from their mamas to always be alert for threats. Their eyes, ears, and noses were always testing for the unusual, because it might mean danger.

All deer must be ready to flee at the slightest perceived threat. They must learn to ***"sleep well but sleep light because predators prowl at night."*** Mamas taught their babies to sleep in the open, so in that way their vision was not obstructed nor their flight path blocked. It is interesting, too, that the group lies with heads in random directions, probably so there are sets of eyes to see in all directions around them. If possible, in miserable weather they would need to somehow take shelter, maybe even blocking their vision. The old lead doe might lead while thinking, *We do what we must!* Usually, the others would join her into a sheltered place.

Another important lesson was that they all must run with great speed when an adult gives a warning. That warning might come as a loud snort or cough, or by pawing the ground, or simply by fleeing. Bucks have been heard snorting and pawing the ground if a threat is present (…like when the Mitchells' little dog was out in the dark of night with Grandma. Was that snort a challenge or a warning to others? It did make Grandma nervous.)

Fawns were taught to not trust anything. For example, one day Delawna and Dawna were lying in the barn brush patch, when a little skunk came marching toward them, as if nothing was going to stop it, up the path and into the bushes. Its proud striped tail was held high. Dawna and Delawna were resting on that same path. Young Dawna saw the skunk's small size and doubted it would be a problem, so she put her head back down to rest more. Little skunk brazenly kept walking; probably it would have walked straight into Delawna's face.

Grandma happened to be watching intently from her windows and chuckling under her breath, "Now what will happen? Will Skunk spray?" Step, step, step, without even hesitation, the courageous little skunk continued as if intending to bump right into the deer. Grandma wondered, *Is it blind or just arrogantly over-confident of its stinky obnoxious odor?* "Hmmm," she said with a smile, "The skunk's Authority Test!"

Delawna knew better than to challenge the little black and white fellow, so she finally got up and gingerly stepped aside while Little Skunk passed. It was still on the path ignoring the deer. After seeing her mother leave, Dawna moved also, but she did not understand why. ***But it's so tiny! Why did we move for it?*** Perhaps one day she would answer that question for herself.

If it chose to do so, the skunk could spray such a penetrating stench that those nearby would find it hard to breathe, but skunks do not always use their secret weapon. Grandma had learned about their gentle side when watching toward the barn from her kitchen window. She rarely saw skunks but that is what she saw.

To her surprise she saw actions between a tiny skunk and a curious big red yearling calf. Either animal could have hurt the other, but neither got hurt nor even seemed fearful. Both animals bravely began walking toward the other as if hesitant but confident. Straight ahead they walked until the tiny skunk stopped and stood right beneath the calf's nose.

Then both proceeded to touch noses, almost as if a greeting. That was a high lift for the tiny skunk but it never faltered as the calf stretched downward. A tiny black and white skunk and a big red calf seemed a strange pair as they stood nose-to-nose sniffing. After a good long smell at each other's nose, the skunk simply turned and ambled away to the post pile. The calf did not attempt to follow but just watched, with its head up, ears forward, and eyes alert as if thinking,

What was that? Why would I follow that stinker?

Calf just stood and watched for a while but little Skunk did not even turn to look back!

Brave Mule Deer mamas in late summer.
Their hair is messed from nibbling their rumps.
Is that because of ticks on their backs?

The fawn lesson about not trusting humans would have to be taught during hunting season. It was especially important then to not trust those humans holding a "stick" by their side, or a "stick" over their shoulder.

Then there were many "Respect Your Elders" lessons: Adults eat first. Eat only what Mama teaches is good. Do not challenge an adult deer because their front feet will give the young one a good "cuffing." Follow Mama closely so you do not get lost.

There was one lesson Little Buck learned almost the hard way. While up on the hill near the spring, something slithered through the grass, something not seen before, so he went to check it out. Just seeing it was not enough information, so smelling was tried. As the little black nose got close to the snake its long body became a coil, its head raised with mouth open, and its tail shook making a buzzing rattle, while its eyes centered on that approaching nose. This meant nothing to the inexperienced fawn, but its mother saw and in two leaps she had landed with all four feet on the snake. Her sharp hooves stomped, cut, and trampled until there was no life left in that rattlesnake. Little Buck did not know what might have been the consequence for messing with that snake on the hill, but he did know snake actions meant danger.

Never sniff a snake! Never ever ever sniff a snake!

In the fullness of summer, the does took their babies away from the valley to join the other deer, higher in the hills. They moved from place-to-place visiting familiar watering holes and fresh browsing and grazing areas. That was a time of much learning. The fawns learned about forests and meadows and the animals in those. They learned what to eat and what to avoid. They learned where to get water and food and about the many dangers to avoid.

Their mothers were always there for them. However, there were times when their mother butted them away when they wanted to nurse. At those times she might simply raise her front legs, jump over the top of them, and then leave, as if to say *Not now! I don't want to be bothered.*

An important lesson they learned was to run, run fast, run away from anything they did not recognize. Go back to Mama and do not approach the strange creature. There were badgers, cougars, bear, bobcats, coyotes, and many other living dangers. Any of those could kill or harm a fawn. In the forested mountains any of those could appear. That lesson was a big one and a fawn should do everything they could to avoid those "strangers." Run! Run fast! Run back to Mama!

Two more lessons fawns learned that summer were that some deer have big pointed "crowns" on their heads, and some animals have prickly coverings that hurt other animals. However, there were not many of those prickly ones around, but it only took one experience with a porcupine to learn that lesson.

Never ever ever sniff a snake, BUT never ever ever EVER sniff a porcupine either!

Chp. 5: "Many Wild Visitors"

True, Mother Nature has a lot to do with survival of wild babies, but their mothers rarely yield to adversity. Instead, mothers fight a bitter battle to protect their young. A story has been told of a wildfire razing a forest and leaving only ashes and burned remains. Some of those ashes once revealed one mother bird's love. She was found with her babies on the ground beneath her body. She remained as a charred mass of ash, but her babies survived under her ashes. That was truly mother love.

On the other hand, Mother Nature can be more brutal. On a sunny warm day, while appreciating Mother Nature's many gifts, it is easy to think of "her" as a benevolent provider, but is that true? In fact, Mother Nature allows many painful events and only the strong survive. Watch "her children" as Grandma and Grandpa did and you might see some of that misery.

Though summer was an easy time of life for wild animals, it was also a time for reproduction. Many responsibilities come with having families, whether one or dozens of babies. Birds were an example of this, sometimes nesting twice in a summer. One Mama Robin demonstrated great effort at raising her babies. She made a good nest, laid her eggs in that nest in the willow tree, hatched her babies, then worked extremely hard delivering worms to her downy little ones. But some things were out of her control and her life became difficult. (You can read more about her in chapter 10.)

There was another mother who visited the farm, in fact, she raised her babies on the farm and their story also has a very sad ending. This was a mother in the raccoon family but, before telling her story, earlier raccoon stories must be shared. It is unknown whether those earlier raccoon visits were by several raccoons or just one making separate visits to the farm at different times.

It needs to be mentioned that raccoons visited at some point in time when the young Mitchell children still lived at the Five-Acre Farm. One time the Mitchell son and his friend belly-crawled to the inside of the sliding glass door to watch a raccoon eating just outside the door. There they were almost nose-to-nose with a 'coon who came for cat food kept in a dish on the porch. The 'coon just ignored the boys and continued eating as they quietly enjoyed the sight…not sure which gave up first to go their own way, the boys or the 'coon. The boys quietly snickered and enjoyed their close contact with nature. Truthfully, the 'coon show continued for a long time because that furry fellow was very hungry and humans did not want to bother it. All came away from the event better off.

Another evening a raccoon was discovered by its noise at the cat food dish on the same porch, but this raccoon had serious problems. It was the skinniest, most mauled and hungry animal the family had seen.

Guesses would have been that it had been sick, or was sick, or had been in a confrontation with another living creature. Maybe it had been hit by a car. Its tail looked crooked as if it had been injured. Anyway, Grandma overlooked its health and let it eat.

It was silhouetted by the outside light and, because of that brightness, saliva or water could be seen dripping from its mouth. (A symptom that might have meant a serious disease or maybe simply because it was so hungry it was salivating profusely.) Also, books tell that raccoons wash their food before eating. It is possible that raccoon had washed its food in the cat's water dish and that is what the dripping was. Maybe?

Regardless of the possibilities, the 'coon was fed and did not show up again, unless it was part of the wild family which later made its home under the barn of the Five-Acre Farm. At this later time, a board was discovered torn from the bottom of the barn door. That made an opening, which was also partially dug from dirt. It let animals crawl underneath on the side of the barn seen from the house. The hole was left open because of fear that putting a cover over it might trap an animal of some kind until it died. That was not a Mitchell way of doing things, so the hole stayed accessible while humans were watching to see what wild thing might be using it.

Nothing was seen emerging, but about then a raccoon family started visiting the Mitchell house. They were the cutest little bandit-faced babies. It was four babies and probably an adult. They made themselves comfortable where food could be found on the porch and where water flowed down the ditch close behind the barn. They seemed to be arriving from the direction of the barn hole so conclusions were made. The 'coon family must have been living under the barn.

Early one morning Grandpa left the house through the back door onto the porch where the wood box and cat food were kept. He heard a strange sound and looked down to where his eyes were met by many little bandit-eyes looking up at him from inside the wood box. Baby raccoons were there, several inquisitive little ones "just snooping." They were not afraid and did not scurry to get out, but instead they studied this new thing that had come to "their porch." Grandpa left them to leave the porch when they chose to. After that, they were often seen climbing the chain link fence into the yard. Up one side of the fence and back down the other was an easy action which they did often.

Grandma and Grandpa did not plan for what to do if the 'coons stayed until adulthood. A whole family of 'coons residing under the barn might have been quite a problem. It turned out to not be a problem, though. Other humans changed that on one of those fall evenings when Grandma was up late after Grandpa had gone to bed. After darkness, a loud automobile of some kind roared past the front of their house. The car stopped suddenly just nearly over the culvert pipe which carried water under the road from the hill to the little stream behind the farm's barn.

At this time of year there was only a small amount of water in that culvert, but the culvert did make a good place for raccoons to walk through. They used it to get to the other side of the road from the farm to the hill and possibly back. That was probably their most often used route to the hill, because in the culvert they stayed hidden and cars on the road would not be a threat.

But one carload did see them. After a quick stop with the vehicle lights shining brightly, the car doors quickly opened on both sides and humans leaped out. Loud male voices yelled words implying that they were after something. To the culvert they rushed with guns and flashlights. With their car lights still on, they could easily see, although it was a very dark night. They were hunters on a hunt and the only thing hunted logically would be the raccoon family. The 'coon family had probably first been seen in the light of their car headlamps outside the culvert as the hunters had come speeding down the road.

Grandma watched from inside the Mitchell's front door and listened with a heavy heart, but she did not know how to stop the action that was about to happen. She had turned on the front porch lights, but that did not stop anything. Bad things did happen! Loud guns banged outside the culvert and echoed as they were fired even inside that "metal trap, the culvert." Obviously, humans with guns were trying to kill some small animal hiding inside the culvert. When finished, the "hunters" jumped into their vehicle and roared away, laughing, loud-voiced, and obnoxious, as if it had been a great hunt, funny to see and fun to do.

The next day the scene was heartbreaking for the old couple who had enjoyed the little 'coon family. Several little dead bodies were strewn inside and outside the culvert. The 'coon family had been killed for no reason other than just a thrill to kill. Grandma could not understand how killing could be a thrill, but that was the end of the whole raccoon family. It was up to the Mitchells to "pick up the pieces" and go on with their lives minus the entertainment of those little bandit-faced babies.

This story was about the mother raccoon whose family had a sad ending, even though she had been a good mother. After that, even for many months later, raccoon bones and parts were sometimes washed from the culvert by the power of water coming down from the hill. Each part found brought with it a sadness that humans could do such a thing just for their own gratification, or whatever their cause was for the "raccoon killing episode." Grandma prayed, "Please, God, give all humans, kind hearts. We need a world of peace! Animals need a world of peace!"

Big-un, Little-un, Dawna, and Little Buck with their mamas were frequently joined by other Mule Deer families as they moved from place-to-place visiting familiar watering holes and fresh browsing territories. The young ones often played their chase games and did their deer dance. Those were nature's games to benefit them by making them agile and faster if chased by an enemy. They did not know the serious side of their play. They only knew its delight while thinking,

You can't catch me!..I'll dodge through the bushes and beat 'ya'!

After tiring from play, the fawns rested together, or perhaps went to their moms who were waiting nearby. They were still babies in mind, even though their bodies were growing rapidly. It still felt good to have their mother's warm milk, to feel her soft tongue caress and clean them, to know her constant presence as they slept, to know she would be there for them in any time of need. Anyone watching them together could see their mother and baby affection.

One doe was once observed leading her twins away from the Five-Acre Farm, but the fence she was following was one which her fawns obviously could not get through, over, or under. The doe could have easily jumped it, but instead she just kept walking while they followed until she found a spot where the wires were sagging. At that point the doe jumped over and progressed away. It seemed clear to Grandma the mother deer was thinking about how her babies could manage to get to her if she crossed the fence. That is exactly what happened. Doe jumped over the fence and babies followed by going through the sagging wires where she had led them. Was that doe Twin Mama? Maybe, but regardless, that mother was taking good care of her babies. And, yes, deer do think! They think about how to care for their babies, and other serious situations in their lives.

When the next year's fawns are born the doe turns her attention to her new baby (or babies), then crankily fights away her last weaned fawn. Grandma witnessed that as a doe was grazing inside a small enclosed area. Her young one wanted to get inside to her, but she must have been weaning it because she bared her teeth and raced toward it with hoofs ready to strike if it did not leave. Baby raced up and down the fence to get to her, but she repeated her determined attack. She needed to be free to serve her newborn fawn(s) and the one weaned needed to learn to take care of itself.

She was teaching it to "grow up." That, too, is a hard lesson for a fawn. This little fawn eventually went out of its mama's sight and laid down, but it knew where she was.

Even Twin Mama's yearling, previously dubbed Adolescent, kept showing up now and then as if to see his mother. But his mother had weaned him and she was busy raising this summer's pair. She did not give him much attention, and even forced him away. You might say he was just a little "forked horn," but he really was not. He did not have the two points on each side as is typical of a "forked-horn." The antler on his right was just a single spike sticking straight up, though the left side held double points. (Webster dictionary calls those points "tines," but many people call them "spikes" or "points.")

Grandma watched the yearling and noted his ineptness in everything. He was clumsy. He was curious. His antlers seemed an obstacle as he moved through the brush. He did foolish things like climbing onto the post pile, an unstable stack of various scrap lumber pieces, and sheets of tin. He seemed insecure about himself while relating to other deer. *Just like a teenager,* Grandma thought, while nodding her head. She talked to him, though she was still in the house, "You, Adolescent, are well named!"

Being a teacher for thirty years gave Grandma much experience with children. She knew about the behavior of youth as their bodies change and they must learn to understand those changes. Boys often tried actions which their bodies could not yet do and they became confused. That is the way "Adolescent, the deer" behaved. Much confusion!

Young girls also go through periods of confusion and insecurity, but theirs is usually less obvious, less bold. Is that also the way it is with young does? Are they less bold? Grandma did notice less courage in the female fawns. An example would be the closeness between them and their mothers while the little bucks were more willing to venture away from their mother, and explore.

**Adolescent and two fawns
enjoy apples beneath the barn bushes
and the old apple tree.**

One day Adolescent was seen down in the barn brush patch giving a small bush a hard rubbing with his weird horns. The tiny bush just wiggled away from his pressure unlike what mature bucks do to get rid of velvet in the spring after their new antlers had developed. Velvet is the protective skin-like surface which covers newly grown antlers. Maybe Adolescent had seen big bucks do that rubbing on more solid wood, or there was some other reason for his actions. Maybe there was maturity discomfort, or an itchy horn. Who knows? He did look silly though, mauling that bush.

Adolescent did not yet understand what a buck's role in life was meant to be. He tried playing mounting games with his mother, but Twin Mama soundly rebuffed him and chased him away. It would not be long before all the bucks battled to fulfill their male role in life, but first they would have to survive that deadly season when their wisdom was pitted against that of humans. That time of death called "hunting season" came in the fall when many wild creatures left to avoid the cold (maybe flew south) and when vegetation started changing and dying.

Definite signs of fall were the appearance of apples and the changing coats on animals. Rabbits turned from summer's brown to winter's white, so they could hide in the snow. Deer acquired a new longer, heavier, darker coat of hair to help them survive the cold of winter. Grandma puzzled about the deer's dark coat maybe being more visible to predators when surrounded by white snow.

Grandpa, as usual, had a scientific answer for that, "Hmmm…black absorbs more heat than lighter colors…prob'ly the long black hair mixed in with other hair is warmer…besides deer hair is hollow so it insulates." He had skinned more than one deer so she knew he knew what he was talking about. He was a science teacher, often teaching Grandma when she did not really want to listen. "You see what I mean?" punctuated many of his conversations and she would just nod.

Many seedling apple trees had grown in unusual places: along the roads, beside springs, near ditches, and in old orchards left from early homesteads. The Five-Acre Farm had only forage and fruit, (some fruit trees were seedlings and some had been planted by Grandpa) but in more remote areas the smell of any sweet fruit called raccoons, bear, elk, skunks, birds, bees, and especially deer.

Fruit season was a hard time for fawns because they had not grown old enough to safely jump over fences, especially the yard fence. Their elders feasted inside while the babies wistfully watched from outside. But sometimes Grandma tossed some sweet prunes or apples, scattering them outside the fence where the fawns could get to them. There were times when young ones got trapped inside the yard fence and became frantic when they saw the adult deer leaving the field. Humans stayed quietly inside, hoping the fawns would not get even more frightened and try to make a fence jump.

Many deer parties were held where the ground offered its apple feast. One evening Grandma watched as the deer "attended a party" behind the barn and under the apple trees. There was a lot of pushing, shoving, pawing, and a whole array of bad manners as the deer vied for "refreshments."

Apples required a hard bite to break off a piece and then slobbers and apple chunks flew. It was not a mannerly sight. Young ones stayed back because they must "submit to their elders" or be pawed by a hard hoof. Wise ones avoided the chaos.

Several does and fawns and the young buck called Handsome (another name given by Grandma) were having quite a "celebration," but three large bucks with many-pointed antlers were afraid. They stayed mostly hidden and watched the others from the far corner brush patch. With darkness they might dare to come closer, but experience had made them wary. They were majestic with their large racks crowning their heads, at least one of them with four points. They would surely be an exciting addition to the party, but they knew better than to become visibly vulnerable. Such was the life of a big buck.

Handsome was naïve and brave enough to be very near the house. He ate petite prunes from within the yard fence. Grandma guessed it was the fawn Little Buck who approached him seeking prunes but was hit by a front hoof with the message, ***"This is mine! Get away you little nuisance!"*** This was one of those times when fawns submit to their elders, so the fawn left quickly probably hoping to sneak back for prunes later.

Grandma grumbled and whispered in one of her many one-way deer conversations from inside her walls, "One Day, Handsome, he will grow a 'crown of many points' and you will wish you had been nicer to Little Buck!" Grandma stayed hidden and watched from behind her curtained patio door. She could not help feeling disappointed by greedy Handsome. "They are animals," she told herself. "But they should be nice to each other!" After that it was not as hard for Grandma to think of the challenges Handsome would probably face when hunting season started. Fear! Much fear! Running and hiding, and sometimes seeing or experiencing death!

For Little Buck, Grandma again felt sympathy. His world had been so filled with rejection! The fawn did stay away from the prunes and the aggressive Handsome. The older buck was confident of his authority and did not share with any other deer. Finally, though, after Handsome had his fill, Little Buck approached those remaining prunes and got a few. He was courageous. He had to be!

Little Buck's time to dine, however, would be short because the herd would soon move on. Then, even though not satisfied with food, he would have to try to find his way out of the yard to follow them quickly. If he did not leave soon, they would leave him far behind and then separated from the herd.

This was probably one of those times when Grandma sneaked out the door on the other side of the house, so she could open a gate for any remaining fawns to safely leave the yard. It was a good thing for the elderly couple to have the animals eat the prunes because, when left there, the fruit aged and made their lawn messy. Some prunes had been given to friends, but many remained for the deer. In this way deer helped the humans and humans helped the deer.

It appeared raccoons also did their part in devouring the ripe prunes. The prunes and broken limbs, which had fallen into the Mitchell yard, looked like evidence of a 'coon night raid. Leaves had fallen among crushed and chewed-on prunes in a way that a tame animal would not do. That is the time of day when raccoons travel and scavenge for food. Raccoons do enjoy fruit and do climb trees for it. Grandma's memory holds a night when a large male 'coon was in the prune tree at her childhood home. It was dark and all were asleep, but their family's cow-dog gave the alarm and the 'coon was chased away.

Chp. 6: "Fall Brings Hunters"

A problem about the deer being around people was their lack of fear, which made them more vulnerable during hunting seasons. The Five-Acre Farm was about three miles out of town, so the land around it was legal hunting territory. Deer probably thought Grandma and Grandpa had not hurt them, therefore the men "with the big sticks" would not hurt them either. The men "with the big guns" would and did. That is known because there was at least one gut pile seen across the road in the field at the north side of the Mitchell home. Also, on a "first morning" of one season a loud "Bang" was heard in that same northern field, which belonged to a neighbor. Grandma thinks she knows what animal died then and there. She believes she knows because of clues regarding a missing mother deer.

Hunting season is an extremely difficult time for deer and each year many hunters take home their trophies––meat and antlers. Some hunters returning home travel with deer (or elk) heads fastened to the front of their rigs to show the world how they "had prevailed." Grandma could not understand how a lifeless, glaze-eyed, tongue out, bloody-necked head, the result of a kill, could be anything to flaunt. How could a hunter's ego be inflated by killing an unarmed, unoffending animal in its own home by use of a varied collection of human devices all created to make killing easier? She told Grandpa in one of her radical moods, "Put a hunter out there barefoot with a club. Then he will have something to brag about!"

Grandpa just nodded his head because he had known the thrill of hunting, but he did not want to argue. Through the years he had grown affection for deer and recently found excuses to not pull the trigger, even though a desirable buck was lined up in his sights. He kept going out with his rifle, as if prepared to hunt, but it seemed more for the social camaraderie than for truly hunting. Grandpa always hunted with friends or family.

There was one time when Grandma struggled with a decision to protect "their little herd." A young man hid himself in bushes beside the road between their house and the hill. The hunter knew deer would be coming down from the hill nightly for their apple feast under Grandma and Grandpa's trees. Sure enough, here the deer came, and they were headed right toward the barrel of the young man's gun.

Grandma could not stand to see what was about to happen, so she yelled at the hunter, loudly, very loudly! "Please don't kill them! They are pets!" All words were said with enough volume to reach deer ears and hopefully scare them back up the hill to safety.

The hunter paused and turned to look at her. Probably he was angry, as he backed out of the bushes. The hunter had been one of Grandma's students, so it was hard for her to do this act against him. The deer saw his movement and heard noises and paused. About then a pickup came down the road and a loud "Bang" sent the deer scattering and racing back to the hill for shelter of the trees. Grandma was never sure where the shot came from, the hunter or the pickup but, regardless of the shot, no deer seemed injured. That was in years past and Grandma did not again face the same dilemma.

Grandpa once told a hunter there were no bucks near when he knew, at that very moment, one was resting in the corral behind the barn. Another time Grandpa had to give a final bullet to a little buck which had been badly wounded and then had fled downhill from the hunter on the hill. The severely injured buck had become entangled in the wire fence of the Mitchells' farm. It just weakly struggled where it would have stayed until it finally died. "You go on to work," Grandpa said to Grandma as he went for his rifle. "I have something to take care of."

It seemed illogical for the area around the Mitchell's farm to be deemed a legal hunting area because it held many small farms and houses. Regardless, it was open for one or more hunts each year. Many houses were within range of stray bullets.

There is such a thing as "Doe Season." When the Game Commission decides deer population is too great in designated locations, they allow hunters to kill does or fawns. If hunters take a "wet doe," meaning one nursing a fawn, then the fawn is left as an orphan. A calloused person might say this is not a big deal, but it really is. "Wet" means the fawn is still needing its mother's milk.

Living without a mother that first winter can result in a slow and painful death for her fawn. There are many hazards for a fawn to face alone…many situations in which "youthful lack of experience can turn into fatal mistakes." In such a situation the killing of one deer is often actually the killing of two animals or, if the doe had twins, possibly the killing of three.

Add to that the "Black Powder Season." In the fall, the Game Commission opened a hunting season near the Five-Acre Farm for any age or gender deer. This hunt was only for muzzle-loaded guns, but it brought many hunters driving their pickups slowly down the road in front of the farm. Grandma envisioned road hunters as sharks with a visible upright fin slowly cruising through water for a kill. That was the hunters' demeanor and she could think of nothing to stop them. Some hunters drove vehicles because then they did not have to do much walking or even leave the valley to hunt.

These "almost town animals" were familiar with and did not fear cars and humans, so they would just stand watching a car and be an easy target. This was the worst time of year to live on the farm, because the family knew death lurked at any moment for their four-legged friends. The stalking vehicles and reverberating booms of guns shattered the air for weeks, reminding the old couple that death for their friendly deer was imminent, death was close.

With the commotion of hunters and the frightened scattered wildlife, deer would rarely be seen on the Five-Acre Farm for many weeks. Instead, deer and other animals were seeking refuge hidden in the forested hills. Grandma and Grandpa kept hunters off their land but, since theirs was such a small piece of property, their protection did not really make any difference. On the hillside north of their farm, hunters often filled their tags. A young family worked that land and they needed meat, so they hunted there and even invited friends or family to come there also. Grandma would not be able to identify the hunters but she knew their reason for being there and they were legally in that place.

When the dreaded Buck Season came Grandma hoped the beautiful bucks were wise enough to stay hidden. Adolescent and Handsome were not yet wise, and they were of the age most often killed. Their innocence would make them vulnerable, especially since they had grown up experiencing humans and had learned to trust them.

That early "first morning" air was sweet with fall fragrances, dried grass, a little smoke from the valley, wild phlox, and goldenrod. Elderberries hung heavy on bushes and a light dew covered the plants and grasses. Mountain Ash foliage was punctuated with round orange berries.

Big bucks there did not know that the young man who worked the land had been watching them and he seemed to know even where they slept. They stood among the does and fawns, which were just rising and beginning to satisfy their morning needs: a little browsing, a little nursing, and a little curious mingling.

"Lord, protect them," Grandma prayed after sunrise on that first day of Buck Season, the most dangerous time of the whole season. It was "most dangerous" for the animals which had not experienced human threats and therefore they had become less cautious. About then, she heard three shots from the hill, muted but distinct. It was as Grandma feared. All but the biggest of those three bucks, which had been wary during the "apple party," were in the open meadow on top of the hill. Nobody told them this was the day they must fear.

(Grandma understood the rest of the scenario and, though not actually seeing it, she believed it to be the way she told others as follows.) The deer were oblivious to anything different about this morning until that loud rifle dropped the three-point to the ground. The bullet hit its mark and exploded the buck's heart. The second shot rang, zinged past the face of a fawn, then buried itself into a second buck. That buck staggered as he disappeared into the trees.

Then hooves beat the ground as the herd fled for cover. There was no organization to it, just a wild frenzied escape into the trees. Perhaps some deer saw the shooter, or shooters, and in panic fled into hiding, and were not seen again. The wounded one was tracked by the bloody trail it left. At the end of that trail the hunter found the wounded buck near death. Another shot rang out as a bullet was fired into the injured buck's head to end its life…the third shot fired probably was the third shot Grandma had heard. Those three shots had penetrated the sweet morning silence and spoke of death.

Fear filled the air. Blood colored the verdant dense forest floor while living wild animals there, of all kinds, knew to run or hide because any living creature might pay the price for not doing so. The sweetness of the wild had been shattered. Beauty of the majestic bucks was ended. The peace of the forest was no longer there, and even bird songs probably did not fill the air for days. Time and the absence of humans is all that would help restore wild peace to that place.

Chp. 7: "Hunter Perspectives"

The three shots heard meant it was a good day for the hunters but a sad day for Grandma. She kept remembering the large-antlered bucks staying hidden behind the bushes during the "apple eating party." Even then they had known they were in danger.

Grandma had a new sense of sorrow because she could empathize with the deer's struggles. Their life was hard without adding this human threat at least once each year when they had to go through this terrible ordeal. She lamented to Grandpa, "Was it not enough they had to be constantly watching for four-legged predators? Probably in the future there will be more seasons added, making a longer time they will be threatened--more fear, more deaths from two-legged predators." Grandpa just nodded, but he was hesitant to criticize.

The evening after Grandma believed the bucks had been killed, she felt very heavy-hearted, so she went to the deck to strum her banjo. That was a way to give herself peace. As she sat and hummed and strummed, color from an especially beautiful sunset blessed the western sky and sent a rosy glow on everything. It was almost as if Mother Nature was trying to make peace in their world. Somehow, among the radiant reds, there were still pockets of blue unchanged by the brilliant warm colors, and even mountains around reflected the setting sun's rosy glow. The purples, pinks, and oranges blended, then phased into darkness almost as if nature was dropping a heavy blanket to cover all light.

Grandma had seen movies do that…give an awesome final scene and then "drop the curtain." Was Mother Nature showing her that the next day would be a better day, the next scene a happier one? Whatever Nature was saying, Grandma knew it was final because "You can't fight Mother Nature," regardless of how much you might wish her ways to be different.

Grandma and Grandpa's families were hunters, but the old couple also had tender hearts about animals, especially their pets. Their pets were usually acquired as free and unwanted by fickle humans, but the old couple did pay for two little dogs. The first was a gift from Grandpa to Grandma when they were young and recently married. The second purchased was a "live toy" found in a pet store.

One pet came to the Mitchell home after they owned the Five-Acre Farm. It was just a stray, a "determined-to-stay" stray! Grandma often took scraps down to the shed behind the barn to feed stray cats, because she and Grandpa were unable to leave any creatures hungry. One day as she opened the door to the shed, she got a surprise. A "meow, meow, meow" (a weak little sound from a hidden corner) greeted her but usually she would hear scrambling noises when strays tried to hide or escape from the shed. This time a tail showed beneath equipment which was always stored there.

Scratching sounds implied movement. Then a little coaxing brought out a skinny calico puss cat. That was just what was needed on the farm! Ha! Probably more kittens. Ha! Ha! Luckily there were no babies with her. To take her as a pet could lead to many complications and expenses. That skinny calico would not accept being rejected, though, so she tried to follow Grandma to the house. That was discouraged many times by "shooing her back to the shed," but eventually Grandma gave up and invited her to follow up the trail.

How would the calico get along with the little miniature American Eskimo, their "live toy," which already had claim to everything and everyone residing there at the farm? Not well, Grandma was certain, since the little white dog always chased cats. His name was officially "Trapper." That name was assigned by Grandpa who chose what he considered to be an Eskimo word which he could easily remember. That official name was required to record him on the National Registry as the son of Adzuki Bean and Snow Shadow. Yes, he was an expensive pet found in the window of a pet store, but he was just too cute to leave there. His white toy-soft hair, short legs, pert ears with pink inside, and a tail that curled over his back made him look and feel much like a toy. He was so tiny a string served as a leash to get him home.

The little dog was named "Trapper" for registration purposes but, since Grandma was the name-giver in the family, she affectionately called him "Fuzzy Butt." That name was her act of rebellion to reject behaving like a prim and proper little old lady. Besides that, the dog was very fuzzy and she spent hours taking him outside at nights for "Butt Business."

The calico, now dubbed Miss Kitty, and Trapper did meet. Trapper chased. Miss Kitty ran and climbed. She came back. Over and over! One day Grandma thought to make Trapper acquainted and friendly with Kitty, so Grandma held him in a way for the cat to stand between Grandma's legs while the dog was held dangled over her. "Nice Kitty!" Grandma tried to convince the dog. What was planned was that the two would get near each other. What was not planned was that Kitty's tail stuck straight up and Trapper took a bite, even before Grandma could counsel them to like each other. "Eeoww!" Miss Kitty took off running away, but forgave him, and eventually their hostile chases became games.

No kittens arrived and Miss Kitty learned she could get human affection by crawling via front or back toward human heads and snuggling there. It worked. She became a much-loved member of the family, and she was entertainment for her fuzzy white pal. She roamed the farm and ruled it. She even ate some of the scraps which had been taken to the shed for strays, in addition to her own special cat food. Even snakes became part of her diet. Grandma feared Kitty might find a poisonous rattlesnake, even though none had ever been seen on the farm. Kitty often caught little less-dangerous snakes and rolled around on top of them, probably as a means of control before deciding to eat them. After she decided she was tired of playing, then she ate only as much as she wanted. Sometimes, she left uneaten snake body parts under chairs startling anybody who sat in those porch chairs.

Would Kitty come back to finish eating them later? Perhaps, unless Grandma found and disposed of them before she came back. Snake pieces were not desired on the porch, just as living snakes also were not wanted on the farm. Really, Kitty did a good deed by protecting from snakes.

**Trapper and Miss Kitty.
It is a standoff,
but she is in control
and he knows it.**

Miss Kitty and Fuzzy Butt brought love and laughter into the old couple's lives for many years. The Mitchells often commented as their pets were ageing, "Wouldn't it be great if dogs lived past their "teens!"

When Grandma drove to town a few days after she heard the guns on the hill, she saw two cloth-covered deer carcasses hanging from the rafters in the shop of the young "hill farmer." She felt certain she knew where these bucks had been killed, and that she had even heard the shots fired which took their lives.

Two happy hunters got their meat that first morning. It was a good hunt for the hunters and then it appeared to be respectful care for the meat. The heart and liver were probably kept clean to be cooked in a special way, and the large antler racks might serve as an ornament on a human wall.

From a human point of view, that was the way it should be but, from an animal's point of view, it was a horrible event. Never would the herd's remaining days be the same. Fawns would have a fear like they had never known before. The big bucks would never reign supreme to make a new set of majestic offspring and, from this time on, all deer in that herd would have to be much more cautious to avoid the two-legged predator.

Family experience had shown that correct cooling and ageing in this way, before cutting meat up, makes it more tender and flavorful. The white cloth bags meant the young farmer was wisely taking care of the meat, as it aged. The carcasses were now a source of food for his family, rather than being the wild animals which blessed the land.

Grandma understood about all of that because her family had been hunters in years past. Her son and husband both had a set of their deer antlers mounted, though the antlers did not hang on her walls. In fact, she had killed a little buck once by herself. It was more an accident than an intentional kill. She did not even know she had killed it.

In her young years of marriage Grandma had generated enthusiasm to join her spouse (the young Grandpa) in "the hunt." She was not an experienced hunter. When she fired at a deer and saw it cross behind a tree and out the other side, she was sure she had missed it. But the young Grandpa convinced her that she got her buck. She did not believe him, until he took her over to the tree and pointed to a little brown body lying on the ground. It was not the animal she had tried to kill. (She had killed a young buck with nubbins not much larger than those of the fawn, Little Buck.) She had killed a baby. *It was a baby! Oh, no! How could I have done that?*

The tears had rolled down young Grandma's cheeks as young Grandpa skinned her kill. She had to hold apart the little fawn's warm legs as her husband cut open the stomach. The little legs were hot to her hands, but seared her very heart. Never again did Grandma fire a shot. Strangely, even if she tried, no bullet would leave the barrel of her gun.

Grandma's family were country people. They either raised their own meat or hunted for it. That was just an accepted thing, and all were happy when a good piece of meat was brought home. However, Grandma was never to be a hunter. Her heart was too tender.

Her family told a story about a buck that would not die – a nearly tragic story. A large beautiful buck with a huge rack was shot and lying on the ground, perceived dead. The hunter leaned his gun against a tree and, with only his knife, approached to cut the buck's throat (a necessity to bleed it out for good meat.) But, while he started to cut, the deer recovered and jumped to its feet. It attacked, wielding its large antlers like many spears. With only the knife in hand, the hunter was extremely vulnerable to the big buck's sharp antlers and hooves. The hunter's fate was probably death, except for protection from his big yellow dog, Nickie, who was always at the hunter's side. Nickie charged between the deer and hunter while barking, snarling, and counter- attacking. He loved his master and was willing to lay down his life for that master.

The hunter was able to get back to his gun as the deer and dog battled, but he was unable to shoot because the dog was in line of fire. Finally, the hunter had to pull the trigger and the deer dropped, but so did Nickie. It was not the bullet that injured the dog, but instead the buck's antlers had ripped his stomach open, letting his intestines hang to the ground. They literally fell out into the dirt and evergreen needle-covered filth.

The saddened hunter was safe, but his faithful dog was in grave jeopardy. Nickie's exposed intestines were pushed back inside by the hunter's hands and held wrapped there by his handkerchief. The hunter held his suffering bleeding dog in his arms and quickly started walking toward home, to their house on the homestead.

No veterinarians were available at their mountain home so "what needed done" had to be done by the hunter and his wife. They washed and sterilized the exposed gut with homemade soap or some other kind of sanitizer. Then they pushed it back inside and sewed the flesh and skin together, using a regular sewing needle and thread, both which had been drenched in alcohol. Nickie must have known to allow their help, though he had to be feeling great pain. There was no painkiller or tranquilizer available for them to use to diminish his pain. Nickie just laid, trusting his master, and let them sew. He had to be motionless and calm to let them work.

Nickie survived the ordeal. The dead buck was retrieved, and the hunter was unharmed because of his faithful pet. Grandma knew that story very well, because Nickie was a part of her life and the hunter was her father. She remembers Nickie as living with their family until "age took him away." He suffered in his older years and finally adults had to agree, "It is time to end his pain." The hunter could not do it, or even know it was being done.so his wife made that decision. A friend solved the problem of Nickie's pain; then the much-loved pet was buried in the soft soil of the family farm. Nickie had spent many years living with his hunter's family, always being treated like a special one of the family. They were grateful when Nickie's pain was over but sad about their loss.

Hunting became less a part of Grandma and Grandpa's lives as the years passed. Hunting is an emotional experience, sometimes an uncomfortable one. Grandma believed there might be a certain anguish felt by all hunters after they killed a living creature, especially if the animal suffered and the hunter saw its pain and heard its mournful cries. Perhaps then a hunter felt regret. If he did not find an animal he had wounded, thus causing it to suffer until its death, the hunter might regret that action. Maybe there were animals injured by arrows, and the arrow might remain in the animal for a time, or until it died. That does happen! Wouldn't that knowledge bother the hunter who caused the suffering?

After the old couple became more aware of the unpleasant possibilities, it was much easier for them to simply get meat from a store than to hunt for wild meat.

Grandma remembers a day when a hunter killed a doe in the field just north of the road toward the hill above their Five-Acre Farm. School had ended for the day. Cars and the school bus were all parked at that location near where the doe had been killed. What a horrible situation that was! Grandma only knew about it because she had started for town in her car and had to wait to drive past the cars and through the chaos of people and animals. There was much commotion with hunters, observers, possibly children on the bus, and little fawns so frantic they were racing around and between the vehicles, trying to get to safety. Maybe the fawns were still trying to get to their mother? All Grandma knew was that the fawns were terrified and running even in places which put them into more danger

It appeared the shooting was done from or near the road, because that is where car(s) were parked on the edge of the road. It was assumed a doe was killed, the mother of two fawns, judging by their frantic race through the commotion. Before Grandma passed it all, the dead deer had been gutted and was being dragged down the hill from the farmer's field to the road. That is what the fawns saw and that must be what brought the deer babies to the road. They did not know which direction to go, toward their mother or away from what killed her. They just ran.

The last Grandma observed, as she finally drove past the commotion, was one little fawn surging alone into a draw, which would give it a place to hide in the trees. Grandma did not see the second fawn again, but maybe it had raced the opposite direction and back onto the hill. That event, which was caused by a road hunter, left many bad memories for those involved. Even worse than memories, was the fact that it left those two little fawns without a mother before they would be facing winter alone.

This happened at the edge of the valley where many homes had been made, where farmers worked the fields, where children played, where pets were in yards and fenced fields, where wild animals had learned they could trust humans. Probably the doe had not even tried to flee with her babies because she felt safe seeing the hunter nearby. For deer this was thought to be a location of safety. It was a sunny grassy field backed by huge pines, other evergreens and edible bushes where wild animals often rested, knowing they had a sheltered hidden escape route behind them.

The problem about this location for the wildlife was that the road, which seemed a separation for the animals as "safe or unsafe," made it possible for hunters to easily see them. Houses mostly sat on the south side of the road, leaving animals the more natural mountainous side. That road was really the dividing line between areas to hunt and those areas for "no hunting."

Perhaps this was a legal kill, but it was not a good choice by the decision maker who caused it to occur. Children were involved. Traffic was obstructed. It was a poor choice regarding wildlife management. And, worst of all was the result when two little fawns were exposed to the situation and probably lost a parent before winter's ordeals. Did the fawns survive the winter? Nobody will know, nor will they know why they died, if death of one or both fawns is the result. Winter survival is hard for orphans.

Chp. 8: "The Herd Returns"

After the big bucks died, not many deer were seen on or near the Five-Acre Farm. They were afraid to be seen and must have moved further back on the hill into the trees. Then eventually, the apple attraction became too strong for the does and fawns to resist moving again into the valley.

When they started returning Grandma was thrilled to see the doe which had the split ear and her fawn called Dawna. Arriving, too, was a doe with twins. Grandma's thoughts were often about the deer. *Was that Twin Mama with Big-un and Little-un? Maybe it is, because there is a size difference in the twins.* Grandma studied each animal closely. The double-single antlered buck was not with them, so Grandma feared for Adolescent. *Did Adolescent die in the hunt? Well, hunting is over so maybe they can have peace for a while.* There were several does with single fawns, but it was impossible to tell if Little Buck and Mama Deer were among them.

Many babies together meant there would be much play, and they did play. The young ones were mature enough their play was fast and wide-ranging as they raced: across the field, through the bushes, down to the corner, over the fence, through the neighbor's field, circle and return to start over again. Now, it seemed to be a competition to prove which was best…and they were good! Grandma was amazed at the ease with which they jumped the fences, dodged through the thorny bushes and over the little creek which drained the spring. They had grown much, and had become very agile from their summer's play.

Mother Nature must have been proud. Her babies were healthy and strong. Her little bucks were courageous, as they should be to create the next generation. Her mother deer were always faithful and leading their families well.

Dawna was a "girly little thing." She stayed close to the split-eared Delawna, so it was easy to tell they were "mother and daughter." Dawna seemed to do things with a delicacy and ease--quite unlike Little Buck and Big-un, who did all things "full throttle." Even her maneuvers to get through or over a fence were done with ease and no wire-snapping. Grandma could almost "see" Dawna think, as she cavorted with the other deer in the fields. Dawna was cautious but not fearful.

It was hard, or nearly impossible, for Grandma to determine the named fawns as they cavorted through the fields. The only clues she had were when they returned to their mothers. Then she could only make guesses because the young ones mingled well with all of the adult animals.

Deer visited the Five-Acre Farm
and enjoyed the
Petite prune tree.

It appeared the does were Twin Mama, Delawna, and maybe even Mama Deer, because the single fawn could have been her baby, Little Buck. Grandma enjoyed watching the fawns' youthful vigor. She understood and remembered motherhood, as she saw the does calmly watching their fawns at play. Grandma's children had matured as she watched them grow and play. She, also, had become an appreciative onlooker as their skills blossomed. Then, even the Mitchell grandchildren matured into beautiful and wise granddaughters. Grandma strongly felt "mother love" and could see that same "mother love" shown by the does for their fawns.

A few days later, the attraction of apples brought even more deer. Two came which appeared to be Handsome and Adolescent. This time Adolescent's antlers were again strange. Just the normal two-point branch antler was on the left, but his right spike was dangling downward by his jaw, floppy and loose. Also, another old bossy doe was in the corral with a sleek young doe, the old one acting greedy and mean. That was understood, by the way she kept striking at the young one each time it tried to get an apple. Grandma again had deer to name… "Greedy and Timid." Timid did not fight back or even leave, but just kept making attempts for food, all which failed. It is possible Timid had been an orphan and had experienced similar treatment all her life, surviving just by persistence.

The season of rut synchronized with apple season, so there was much socializing and much migration of deer as groups, or even as singles. Both does and bucks had an urgent need to find mates. The fawns were mostly ignored during this time. If a buck joined the group, seeking a ready doe by her scent, the fawns had to stay out of the way. They were not welcome. One little buck fawn, identity not certain but maybe Little Buck, did the scent test on his mother then tried to mount her. Of course, the doe angrily chased him away. He was trying to imitate what he had seen. That awareness might serve him well in adulthood, if he survived that long.

Grandma started seeing more bucks around when their fear faded and their hormones took over. It was time for rut and they wanted to breed. Just like sexually promiscuous youth, the bucks lost common sense in their hunt for a mate, wandering around in the open as they hunted. Grandma saw one buck pass through, even ignoring humans, right past the yard fence and across the field with his nose to the ground while walking and sniffing. He never looked right or left to watch for humans, but just used his nose as his guide. He was seeking that "ready doe" by scent.

This was a chaotic time for all the deer, because unwilling does were irritated with attention, willing does went away hunting a partner, and fawns were ignored or literally pushed from the group. Fawns did not understand their being rejected, while for a time they held little importance in the deer world. Fawns were even sometimes abandoned by their mothers for days, because she was involved in "romance." Other times fawns were around when the doe and buck came together, but fawns were chased away from the action to only watch from the sidelines.

This was when Grandma saw the romance between the young twinkle-eyed doe and her suitor (as mentioned in Chapter 3). Time has added familiar members to the herd and now Handsome and Timid match the qualities of this amorous pair.

Outside Grandma's kitchen window, a beautiful three-point buck arrived at the barn brush patch. He looked like the buck she had called Handsome. There were does near the bushes, but he was interested in only one of them. He chased the others away. He pursued his choice, but the one resembling Timid evaded. He chased and she ran, but not too far. Repeatedly, he tried to approach her but her eyes said, *"Maybe I should be afraid."* Over and over this happened, and several times when she started to leave, he blocked her with his body. Being unable to leave, she quit trying to escape and just stood watching him. As Timid would step forward or backward, he would imitate her steps. With her ears forward and big brown eyes wide, her demeanor was "interested curiosity."

Handsome stood a short distance in front of Timid and posed like a motionless statue with his chest held forward, his head held high, his antlers proudly forward, and his neck arched and strong. He looked straight ahead with his eyes never looking her direction, yet he knew what she was doing. He knew she was watching him so he stood strong, still, steady, and proud. For her he was demonstrating his majesty as they both stood frozen to the spot for what seemed a long time. Grandma could almost imagine his body bronzed, because he would have been a beautiful statue. That is exactly what Handsome looked like in his frozen posture for the one he had chosen.

It appeared Timid liked what she saw, but intended to be "hard to get" a while longer, so she turned and quietly slipped into the bushes. If deer can tip-toe, that is what Timid did, as she slowly, lightly, and quietly placed each small hoof onto the loamy soil and sneaked behind the barn into the thicker brush. Hiding did not work for her, though, because Handsome saw and came rushing, noisily crashing into the bushes after her.

That was the last Grandma saw of the romance between Handsome and Timid but, since it was evening and beginning to get dark, imagination can easily fill in the rest of the story. They were not there the next morning.

What Grandma did not know was that the Game Commission had planned another hunt for that area, but later in the season. Black powder rifle hunters needed a special hunt and, as best she knew, it would allow for the killing of **any size or gender deer.**

The Commission did not expect to lose many animals with this hunt, because hunters were handicapped by their guns. Black powder guns were (and still are) old-fashioned ones in which a ramrod was used to stuff a ball and powder into the barrel. There the powder was exploded by a spark from the hammer. Usually only one shot was fired since it took much time to reload the gun.

Black powder was not an easy way to hunt, but good hunters, though in past years, found merit and success with this technique. They still do find it a challenging way to hunt.

That planned Black powder hunt was to be in the exact area where the Mitchell home had been placed. Even the Five-Acre Farm would have been legal for hunting, but Grandma and Grandpa denied hunters use of their land. However, their land was next to legal hunting property, for which they had no authority.

Grandma was concerned about the Black powder hunt, so she went to the office of the Game Commission. She told them about the lack of deer, and the fact that the hunt was going to be right in her neighborhood where people lived and worked. "Shouldn't they keep hunters away from the valley?" she asked. Her questions seemed to not be heard, instead by attitude they were ridiculed.

Officials said the deer there were ample and that the location for the hunt involved more than just the valley. In fact, they said the animals needed to be thinned. They seemed to have official statistics and that was what mattered to them. Grandma's concerns accomplished nothing. The hunt was already scheduled, and that is the way it would be!

According to the officials, this hunt was for White Tail Deer specifically, so Mule Deer should not be a target. However, the White Tail Deer were rarely seen at the valley's edge, so how they could be considered "ample and needing thinned" left Grandma confused.

Grandma's confusion was partly caused by the fact that the road built east and west in front of the Five-Acre Farm was also the boundary for the Game Commission's Hunting Unit (a large designated area to be used according to specific hunting licenses.) That meant hunters could be shooting at animals just across the road, but they might also be hunting much further into the mountains. The road boundary was logical for the Game Commission, but it was not logical for homeowners who lived next to the road. Thinking from a deer's perspective the road probably cost them many lives. (A guess was made by trying to think like a deer.)

During controlled 'Black Powder Only' seasons, there were restrictions on the hunters which did make the hunters' task more difficult. The muzzleloader gun must be the type fired from the shoulder, must be loaded from the muzzle, must be only a single shot (unless in a situation using a shotgun), must not use scopes or sights that use batteries, or artificial light or power, must use only flint or percussion caps, and must use only loose or granular black powder or such substitutes as available for propellants. This gave the deer some advantages. However, those seasons may have typically lasted a long time. One mentioned was from October fifth through November eighth. (The above information came from official documents.)

And that is the way it was! There was a Black Powder Hunt. Grandma could hear the "blunderbuss shots" (a name used for the loud report of a black powder gun) even from the distance on the hill as hunters fired their antique weapons.

Since the distance range for those guns was shorter, some hunters opted for driving down the roads where they could possibly get a closer shot. Also, a vehicle would more easily get the hunters to where they could see animals without being seen. Deer, which were less afraid of humans, would be more apt to stand as easier targets for Black Powder hunters. Those deer living on the edge of town had less fear, and hunters knew that.

Grandma did appreciate that the recent hunters were using a method more like that method used by earlier generations. That type of hunting could not be easy, and it does give the deer a better chance for survival. However, that Black Powder season was a harder one on the Five-Acre Farm family. Sounds of the many vehicles cruising the road north of their house, and fear for animals who had become like friends, permeated the old couple's days. It seemed that season lasted for a very long time. It seemed the cruising vehicles with hunters driving slowly were never going to stop passing by. They would even park or turn around at the road corners to extend their vision of that hillside, The hunters were like sharks in water which cruise and persist until they get their prey. The old couple knew the "sharks' prey" could be one of their "four-legged friends."

Chp. 9: "Black Powder or Doe Season?"

Deer and elk both lived in the nearby mountains but elk were never "friendly neighbors" like the deer. If elk knew humans were near, they always seemed to speed away. Perhaps they were too smart to trust humans. They were fast as they fled from human sight so, even if they had been there, humans probably would not know it.

Elk hunting season was also held in that area north of town, but elk were not often seen that near the valley. When traveling toward the valley, elk usually crossed the tree-covered butte which could be seen from the Mitchells' kitchen window. Then, after crossing the butte, elk mostly went directly to the north and out of sight on the hill. The Mitchells did not often see elk near their farm, but there was one time which was a very memorable experience! The couple were standing nearly in the middle of an elk herd even though the herd was quite close to their Five-Acre Farm.

Grandma and Grandpa had taken a walk down the road, over the rise, and toward the butte. They took Trapper, their little dog, with them. He was kept on a leash to hold him close while they were walking down the often-busy road. It was an evening walk so the road was mostly untraveled. It was a good time to enjoy nature, but things changed quickly. Nature came to them! They had not seen any elk until they were returning home just at the rise. As they topped up, they saw a herd of elk leaving the north hill and crossing the road directly in front of them.

The couple also saw some of that herd in their neighbor's field. The elk were jumping the fences on both sides of the road to get from the hill into that field south toward town. This put the animals between the Mitchells and their Five-Acre Farm. Grandma, Grandpa and Trapper were just topping the little ridge for the downhill part of their walk so they were surprised to see a big bull elk in front of them. It was facing away from them and standing in the middle of the paved road. The bull just stood there. It seemed to be slowly considering what to do next. It was not aware humans were standing close behind him, while quietly watching him.

The wind must not have carried the scent of humans to him, and the watchers were silent and motionless. The bull held his big horned rack high and paused, while standing on the mid-road yellow line. He simply scanned the hill and the fields as the herd was passing in front of him. Many elk were crossing the road and mostly leaping over fences while headed south into the neighbor's field. The bull elk stood, for what seemed like a long time, just watching the others, while humans and dog also stood quietly observing the big animal and all the herd scattered on both sides of the road.

It was an impressive sight for the Mitchells, lasting until some elk in the field discovered human presence. Then all of them started running back to the hill. They were escaping from the open field, back across the road to the hill, and there to the cover of trees. In fear the excited herd jumped over or tore out wires of fences on both sides of the road. The big bull joined them as they fled back to hidden safety.

It was a frantic large herd of elk which plunged as a mass back across the road while people and pet quietly stood and watched the wild commotion. Surprisingly, little Trapper also stood very still and watched (as if he understood the need for quiet) until he was led calmly back home. That elk show had been just a short distance from the farm. That happened in the fall near the time of rut for elk, a fact which might explain their many-bodied migration.

The elk rarely were seen that close to the Five-Acre Farm. Hunting seasons for elk had little effect on those people living in town, or even those near town like the Mitchells. Hunters did come, but most elk hunters went out to the forested mountains to hunt that big game. There were often several seasons each fall for hunting elk like those seasons for hunting deer. The main chaos hunting seasons caused was the influx of hunters, which in many ways pleased the local business owners. Though elk seasons varied, Grandma believed there were seasons for hunting cow elk, spike elk, and full-antlered bulls. The elk babies maybe had to "dodge bullets," and some elk calves may have lost mothers. Fall and hunting seasons caused the herds to separate and hide for their safety. Then the elk became much more nervous about being seen.

Grandma and Grandpa often took summer drives to the forested northern hills just to see what game they could spot. There were times when both deer and elk were seen, but usually only in small numbers. To the contrary, large herds of elk were occasionally located and were just visually enjoyed–no hassle, no hunting. It was fun to see how many elk the old couple could count in those herds, and sometimes the numbers were even in high two digits.

On one of those mountain driving trips with another couple, life did not seem normal. There was a herd of cow elk and their yearlings in a meadow. The couples saw one cow elk give birth while they quietly watched from distance in the car. The cow did not get up to step away into the trees as many of the others did, but remained prone on the ground for a while. Then, when she finally did get up, a tiny calf elk managed to get up beside her. Both were standing and the mother was trying to coax her baby away toward the trees. Baby moved a few steps then the humans left.

In that herd there were very few babies with the many cow elk resting in the meadow. There were, though, many last year's calves with the cows and some were even nursing on their mothers. Last year's calf would not be allowed to have its mother's milk, unless she had no baby from this year to nurse her. But, if she had no current baby, then why did she have milk? Is it possible predators had killed the new baby elk, in the way that the mother bear had killed the newborn baby deer? (Chp. 2, pg. 9 of this book).

Grandma had some confusion about seasonal game hunts, deer hunts especially. She believed some years there was a Doe Season, sometimes a Black Powder Season, and yearly Regular Buck Seasons. Some seasons were specifically for White Tail Deer. It was not certain in which of these hunts this following story occurred. Most logically it was Doe Season, since sometimes there were special doe hunts held to reduce numbers in certain farming locations. Several hunts had been held in the same year in the same area where the Mitchells lived. This served to increase the number of "two-legged predators" hunting during fall.

It was in this chaotic time of hunting when Grandma heard one loud rifle discharge up on the hill, and she saw fawns racing down toward the Five-Acre Farm. One little wild-eyed fawn came darting across the road and through the open gate before it realized Grandma and Fuzzy Butt were standing right where it was headed--to the barn and the sheltering brush patch. In more fear the fawn spun around and found a hiding place back in the bushes at the hill side of the road.

The frightened fawn was soon joined by several other fawns and does, also racing down from the hill. The little group nervously moved in and out of the bushes, but mostly kept their eyes centered on the area on the hill from which they had fled. Their legs did a frantic fidget, while their cupped ears were erect and held pointed toward that same location so any sound clues could be heard. Their nostrils flared as they tried to reap clues from the air, seeking scents that would tell them what had happened or what might yet happen.

A hunter had found them, but Grandma did not know the result of that hunt. The little herd tried to reach the place which they had known as a safe-haven. They must have known that one animal from their herd was somehow hurt by a hunter. The question for Grandma was which one might have been lost to the hunter's shell.

There was no way to know exactly what had happened on the hill. The deer themselves gave clues by their frantic behavior. The several nervous deer eventually moved away from the other side of the road and toward the Mitchells' barn. They stayed near the barn brush-patch for a while as if hiding and gaining courage to leave that place which they felt was safe. When calmed, they did not go back to the hill but chose to migrate the opposite direction, through the fields to the south. They seemed to stay together even after they left the farm. While they were gathering their courage at the farm, Grandma studied them for answers to the many questions she then had.

Grandma had watched closely to find clues about which deer might have been killed by the hunter. She did see Delawna and Dawna and was relieved. "There they are, Grandpa!" She happily pointed to the deer, "See the split ear." Three fawns stayed near Delawna. Does rarely, if ever, give birth to triplets, so that must mean there was one or more mother deer missing. *It must have been one doe which the hunter killed, leaving only one fawn,* Grandma decided.

Two of those three fawns could have belonged to Twin Mama, and the lone fawn could have belonged to Mama Deer. *Is it possible two does were killed leaving three babies as orphans?* Grandma puzzled, then remembered she had heard only one shot.

There was no way to know which doe was the actual mother of the three fawns. More information was needed, but Grandma concluded, *It must have been one doe which the hunter killed, leaving only one lone fawn.* In that frantic little herd of deer there were no bucks, but there was one lone fawn now without a mother.

Is this Little Buck,
or Orphan, or is it both?
It is undoubtedly alone!

The little group would usually spend some nights in the barn brush-patch, and then they would be gone again early the next morning. It seemed nature's way to protect them was by keeping them from loitering a long time in one place. They probably needed to keep moving to stay ahead of predators, because when their scent became strong it was a clue about deer presence for their enemies.

It became clear there were not enough does for the fawns in the nervous group, so surely a doe had fallen to the hunter's rifle. Grandma could not be certain which doe was missing, but since there was that extra fawn with Delawna and Dawna the possibility was ominous. Has Mama Deer been killed? Did Little Buck lose his mother? Is he an orphan? Those questions might never be answered with certainty, but Grandma kept gathering clues.

Sometimes there were more deer than the usual group, and sometimes there was only a doe with her twins seen. Yes, the twins were big and little, so they were probably Twin Mama's family. Occasionally, with them were the nervous Handsome and silly Adolescent, whose loose spike horn no longer dangled, but was totally gone. However, there was never a pair that resembled Mama Deer and her baby, Little Buck. An extra fawn often seemed to be in the group, but no special markings made it identifiable as Little Buck. After this episode, Twin Mama and Delawna often had an extra fawn traveling with them (near but not nursing).

Fall also brought many wild turkeys which started feeding on the hill. Probably they roosted nights in the tall pines, and then fed on the hillside and fields during the day, while sometimes passing through the Five-Acre Farm. Their number was huge, because they now had their summer broods with them.

Once Grandma saw about twenty turkeys sauntering curiously and cautiously down the lane toward her house. Their steps were punctuated by subtle curious words, "**Churk? Churk? Churk? Churk? Churk?**" If Grandma had not stopped their travel, those turkeys would have had a flower-bed feast.

"Shoo! Shoo!" Grandma raced toward the turkeys while flapping her arms, causing their big wings to take flight and carry them away over her head. From underneath, she saw their small heads and necks stretched forward and their legs pulled up and backward, like airplane wheels after the plane's heavy body leaves the ground. She heard the loud "swoosh" each time a wing thrusted downward, pushing for lift. It required a lot of strength to propel their heavy bodies through the air.

They had been designed to only make short flights, but long enough distance to escape predators--long enough to get away from Grandma. Also, they needed flight to get into their roosting trees. Only there would they be safe from threats found on the ground. (This need for flight to safety must be the reason the young poults learned to fly so quickly.)

If turkeys sleep in trees, then comes the question about protection while turkey hens are nesting on the ground. That is where a hen must nest because her babies would not be able to manage flight from a tree nest. Mama hen turkey must simply nest knowing she and her babies are in jeopardy. She has no major defense, if a predator attacks or tries to steal her eggs, except perhaps a strong flogging with her wings, and those toes do have sharp claws on the ends of them. An assumption can be made that a hen turkey would fight to the best of her ability against any attacker. (Would the attacker be a tom turkey trying to destroy her eggs? Maybe.)

Wild turkeys were usually not welcome at the farm because in large numbers they destroy yards, gardens, and flowers and then leave excrement on everything. If they find birdseed meant for other birds, it would be voraciously devoured and invite return visits. Grandma and Grandpa did enjoy watching the turkeys, but only from the distance. Since there were hundreds living in nearby fields and hills, turkeys could have been overwhelming if they had decided to do anything besides just pass through the Five-Acre Farm. Turkeys and deer both made their presence known near the farm.

******

One warm fall morning, after the first snow had fallen and quickly melted away, a troop of about eight deer was enjoying the lawn-like grass in the field in front of the Five-Acre house. The sun was warm and surely the newly "watered" fall grass was sweet as the deer calmly nibbled the green delicacy. Even the fawns seemed to be enjoying the tender new growth in this place which felt like safety to them. (Since turkeys sometimes crossed or rested at the Five-Acre Farm, perhaps turkeys considered it in the same way, "like safety")

Grandma studied the group of visiting deer. She saw Delawna (with the torn ear), and Dawna who was probably one of the young ones of varied sizes. Grandma noticed a limp when the smallest young one moved. "Oh! No!" Grandma exclaimed as if in personal pain. "Her ankle! Oh! … No!" The left rear ankle was so broken it made the little foot flop sideways. The little deer hobbled forward but still ate–it had to eat because hunger is a survival skill. "How can it stand the pain?" Grandma sadly urged, "Come look, Grandpa, Oh! Look!"

"Yup! Too bad! Can't fix deer like they do people…Game Commission would just shoot it," replied Grandpa in his stoic manner when he saw the fawn's injury. That was probably true, since they had seen officials stalk a doe with a broken leg near the state highway. The old couple assumed that doe would be shot when they saw men in uniforms encircling it in the field next to their town. Since it was near the road, logic would say it had been hit by a car on that highway. The injury appeared to be severe enough that it could not be fixed, not on a wild animal.

Grandma agreed with Grampa about the seriousness of a leg injury. In deep thought she rubbed her head and mumbled, "So, what do we do about the little fawn? If we report it, they will kill it! If we don't report it, then it will continue suffering! Oh! Which?"

They chose to let Mother Nature solve the problem. There was nothing else they could do, but afterward there was a pall over the Five-Acre Farm with sadness for the little injured fawn.

The Mitchells had decided the injury was on the littlest one of Twin Mama's babies. Confusion was added when other fawns passed through with only small symptoms of a leg injury. Their legs were closely studied to learn if it was Little-un. This left the old couple hoping Little-un was improved, but doubting such quick healing of that terrible injury which they had seen before. They even questioned the fawn's survival.

Chp. 10: "Mama's Faithful Care"

Each time a fawn was seen, its legs were closely studied to see if it was Little-un. Surprisingly the little fawn did survive but, each time they looked, it was still limping because of its foot problem. "That foot is still flopping sideways…Oh, how can it possibly heal?" Grandma repeatedly lamented, though Grandpa often was not even in the room to hear.

With closer watching, Grandma often guessed any limping fawn was Little-un, the smallest of Twin Mama's babies. This guess was from the fact that the other deer moved on, but the doe with the large fawn and the small injured fawn stayed at the farm. Twin Mama must have known her injured baby could not travel, so she stayed where its needs could best be met. Other deer moved through the field, mingling then leaving. Twin Mama mostly stayed within the borders of the fence with her babies.

The three browsed on bushes and even grazed on the field grasses. They slept in protection of the brush patch and beside the little stream flowing from the culvert. Little-un managed to move around, although her hoof seemed almost unattached. She still ate and tried to stay with her family, but now and then it was noticed that she would be acting as if her injury was hurting.

Twin Mama and her family were breaking a survival rule by staying there in one place behind the barn. It was a place they had previously known for safety. Often their ears and eyes would be studying the house during daytime, or even as they remained in their night beds after Grandma and Grandpa were up in the morning. *Funny--they study us as much as we study them,* Grandma thought.

They were there each morning, one big and two little sets of visible erect ears catching the sounds, although their bodies were hidden in the tall grass. Those ears were probably the reason they got their name, Mule Deer. Being like a mule's ears, those ears were large and could rotate far around so they could pick up more sounds. Their ears had a fringe of black hair and another of white; those ears seemed almost to be framed making the total a pretty work of art by Mother Nature. Also, toward the end of their black noses there was a sprinkling of white hair, much like many mule noses. Perhaps, that was part of the reason for their name. However, the small white bib under their chins, and the white tail-centered "bustle" on their rump, had nothing to do with mule similarities. Nor were mule qualities in their short white tails with tips so totally black they looked as if dipped in a bucket of black paint.

Big-un was a beautiful example of what a Mule Deer should look like. Grandma was not certain, but she was guessing, that it was a male and the small twin was a female.

Little-un's small size might have also been a diet problem, and now, since food was harder for her to get, she seemed even tinier. Grandma shuddered to think of how difficult winter would be for a fawn so badly handicapped.

As the three fed and wandered around the Five-Acre Farm, Grandma and Grandpa often studied the injured one's leg from the distance. Grandma's thinking went like this: *Is it better? Is it still broken? Can it mend itself just by walking on it? Or does her movement of it make its bones separate worse? Is there some way to put a cast on it? Naaahhh, that would keep her from being able to lick it clean, and probably then infection would take her life. Just leave it to Mother Nature and pray to Father God!*

Often the injured hoof flopped at a distorted angle, looking just as damaged as it was originally, but sometimes the fawn seemed to put her weight down on it in a straight position, and then there was hope. Otherwise, the little deer just hopped on three legs and appeared to not put weight on the fourth leg. That seemed an impossible injury to overcome, but she had survived for many days and nights. She was only with the other herd deer when they were at the farm because Twin Mama kept her family within the borders of the Five-Acre Farm fence.

There were times when Little-un seemed to be nibbling on the injured spot. Perhaps it was itching like human injuries do when they heal, or maybe it was hurting--a thought Grandma struggled not to consider. There was the possibility that the fawn had stepped on a stick, which penetrated her leg and looked like bone. If a foreign object could be pulled out it might heal, but how could humans do that? That little wild animal could not even be caught. There was no way to be certain about the condition of the wound. Even binoculars only revealed slightly the seriousness of the wound. Grandma tried to avoid seeing the actual injury, since nothing could be done for the fawn and seeing the injury made her human heart extremely sad. It was a good thing Grandpa could distract his wife.

Grandma and Grandpa had been married nearly fifty years--long enough to understand how important it is to have a mate. There is such comfort in having someone to share the "ups and downs of life," someone to be there when medical needs must be faced, someone to comfort during grief, someone to help reason out a problem, someone to share successes, burdens, special pleasure, and joys. It is good just to have someone to make noisy sounds that comfort with the message, "You are not alone!"

Humans like having human company. Likewise, birds and other mammals like having company of their kind. Monogamous mating in the animal world seems unique to mankind, but some other animals develop that male/female bond.

It is said Geese mate for life, and upon death of one, the other never mates again. Grandma believed Doves might also have that bond, because she studied a pair which came to the farm.

Those Doves shared the duties of parenthood. Often, just one baby was hatched in a nest in the east brush patch. "Here I am. Here I am. Here I am." Was that a love song, a lullaby, or just a sweet "Goodnight" crooned to the world as the mellow evening call came nightly from the high electric lines or nearby fence-post? As darkness fell the Doves furtively sneaked into their high bushy nest. It was the same spot nightly, so it must have held their nest.

The Dove parents both seemed to care for their young, then soon three would visit the seed dish, until later in the summer when their extended family again united. The seed pan often fed many Dove guests, and the old apple tree often held their many gray shapes ruffled and preening in the morning sunlight.

There was one morning when an adult Dove was seen teaching a less-than-skilled young one about flight and landings. The adult would fly to a distant tree, and then give its summoning call. (That had to be what the call was, because the call brought the young one to that same tree where it then lit on a nearby limb.) The adult Dove did that repeatedly, as if teaching the young one to answer its parent's call. Maybe it was practicing flying and landing as well, but it certainly was learning to be obedient, since "the game" involved many practice flights.

Being a peaceful beautiful bird, Doves stole Grandma's heart and brought her pain when one day she saw one of them at her feet lying in the grass, where it had just dropped. A vehicle's loud motor was heard racing down the road, so that was surely how the Dove had been injured–a collision between bird and auto. The little blue-grey body's warmth and slightly closed eye lids meant the injury had just happened and that it was a serious one.

When the Dove didn't flinch to Grandma's touch, she gently lifted it to her chest, held it to her heart, and said a silent sad prayer, then mentally grieved, *Why would something so beautiful, so gentle, so peaceful, get so hurt?* Sometimes Grandma would be angry at the blatant selfishness of humans, the thoughtless way many dealt with other living creatures. Humans often drove with reckless abandon leaving injuries or death in their wake. Many deer were victims of thoughtless drivers. Many deer were hurt even on the road in front of the Five-Acre Farm. Their carcasses remained at the side of that road until nature "devoured them," or someone hauled their body away.

Grandma's tender heart often hurt, this time no less than other times, as she held the Dove's warm body until it no longer was warm, no longer was flexible, no longer had any flicker of life. Then it was placed where nothing could damage it more.

That evening a single Dove perched on the electric lines at the road's edge north of the farm. It cooed repeatedly a song which sounded to Grandma's ears like, "Where are you? Where are you? Where are you?" Then, when it got no answering response, it flew a small circle as if to get attention, landed again and sent its song, "Where are you? Where are you?" Over and over, it did this little routine, as if nervously waiting for its mate.

The next day a single Dove ate at the feeder and then after several days it simply disappeared. Were there untended eggs being damaged by the cold, or was an adult with them? Did the lonesome Dove lose its mate forever and leave? Grandma only knew what she saw, and she hoped soon there would again be a Dove family at the birdseed pan.

A couple weeks later two Doves settled on the high electric wires in front of the house when the afternoon was calm beneath overcast skies. The cool air seemed pregnant with rain, which was not yet there. They and other birds knew it was coming, though, and began a dialogue of celebration. Birds seem far better at weather prediction than humans, perhaps because their survival depends on it.

If you have ever watched birds seek shelter when buffeted by a strong wind, you would understand their need for preparedness. Anyway, those two doves seemed to be having a conversation or perhaps just speaking to the world, "Comes the rain. Comes the rain. Comes the rain." Then together the two flew overhead to the nearby willow tree and from there again cooed their song, "Comes the rain. Comes the rain." (Did this mean the lonely Dove found another mate? Grandma believes it did!)

A rush of wing sounds filled the air as smaller birds flew to those locations which they must have believed would protect them from what they sensed would be an attack by nature. The air seemed to be filled with "urgency" as they seemed to know danger was near.

"You're wakin' my baby! You're wakin' my baby!" scolded another different bird from a nearby perch.

"Cheese, Cheese, Cheese," chirped another (perhaps a dumb one) from a different direction while the blackbirds silently, almost frantically, searched Grandpa's seeds for just the right morsels to be satiated before the storm arrived.

Another summer morning while lying in bed, Grandma realized two Doves were perched on the electric wires next to the road and beyond her window. She wondered how they could perch on electric wires and not get electrocuted. The sweet morning air, wafting through her open bedroom window, carried their two-syllable call to her as they did their high-wire act, "Waaaaake-up, "Waaaake-up." Could it be they have a morning song? Their usual sound from that same perch was three syllables sent to be interpreted in whatever way Grandma wished. Maybe it was "Be-care-ful," or "I-love-you," or "Look-up-here," or "Watch-me-fly. All these were new thinking because the mellow song came from gentle Doves which seemed to always be looking at her. They never perched facing away. Grandma could not help wondering, *Is this a message from someone in that great hereafter, a message delivered by a bird.? Why do twenty-four Doves often perch in the willow tree watching and listening to me play my banjo? And why did I see about thirty Doves all perched on the fence at that remote cemetery where we visited one day?*

Those Doves were all lined up on the fence silently watching like sentinels guarding the quiet graves on the still hillside. Human presence seemed only to be interesting to them, but not something to fear. They made no noise except a little whisper of wings as they changed resting places on that wire barrier which was there to keep the unwanted outside. They truly did feel like guardians for those souls resting in the graves.

The Mitchells noticed that Doves collect as families. Where there is one or two, there often is a collection of several birds. It seems they travel in flocks. Perhaps they form family groups or maybe it is just that they are drawn to the same sources like food, water, safety, and other interests.

The one thing, though, they had to avoid was the hawk. Hawks just perched nearby and, if a Dove flew, then it was a race for the Dove's life. The hawk was a much faster flyer and could even catch a flying Dove in its claws and carry it to the ground. Once in the hawk's claws it would not escape. Feathers would remain as clues to the end of that race.

It should also be noted that hunters sometimes would spread bird seed as bait to get Doves to land. There the hunter would wait with a gun loaded and ready for their visit to food. A Dove's life has many hazards.

Dovey and Al.

They are mates

It was easy for Grandma to believe Doves have human personalities, so Grandma named this pair Dovey and Al (The name "Al" for Albino because he was white rather than the typical grey.) Al was so attached to Dovey they were usually just inches apart (hovering close together, a little like some married couples.) Even when Dovey flew, Al also took flight by the same route and landed by her side on her chosen limb.

One day while both were perched on the yard fence, Al leaned forward, closely studied Dovey's face, then pecked her "smack on the beak." It looked like a kiss. (Yes, Grandma knew that sounded like "stretching the story" when told to others, but it was true.)

Dovey and Al's attachment seemed to prevail since, even after many days, they made morning visits to Grandpa's seed pan very close together. Al sometimes followed her so closely he even stepped on her tail- feathers as they pecked for seeds. They were even seen by a neighbor as they were flying to a nest behind the neighbor's barn. Their "attachment" was not without troubles though, because some other Doves were often seen as a flying gang chasing Al. Around and around, they chased with him flying in the lead until all of them finally flew "off into the wild blue." Is it possible Doves have a color bias? Perhaps it was because his feathers were white with black, though the gang and Dovey had grey with brownish feathers. They were from a different "brood"! Al did seem like a larger bird than Dovey.

Could Al have been a different kind of Dove, or maybe there was really such a thing as albino mutations in birds? (There can be albino mutations in humans. The unusual coloration of extreme white is sometimes in human genes to be passed on. That did happen in one family of Mitchell friends.) Grandma might never know what the situation was with Dovey and Al, but in later years she has seen groups of Doves which were mostly white, though in other ways they did resemble Dovey. Hmmm???

Grandma knew Doves were a very special bird since God honored them several times in His Text. It was a Dove which Noah sent to determine if the flood-waters had receded making dry land for The Ark to rest on. It was a Dove, or a Dove-like messenger, which came to Jesus' shoulder when He was baptized by John. Doves were being sold in the Holy Temple when Jesus cast out the money changers, and other evil-doers. Also, when Jesus was born some say there was a Dove watching in the stable from the rafters. And don't forget...... Angels fly!

Dovey and Al certainly were a unique pair who brightened Grandma's days with their frequent visits to the seed pan and yard fence. Their demeanor and graceful flights always demonstrated absolute gentility. It was often the Doves which awoke Grandma in the mornings and cooed her to peace at night. Their sweet presence brightened Grandma's days and their call will stay with her as a song of love forever. It upsets Grandma to know they are on the hunters' list as prey to be shot. (One newspaper reported twenty-five can be legally killed at a hunt).

In all seasons Grandpa kept food available for many "bird friends," though seed was not "cheep" (a fun pun). His special affection went to the little top-knotted Quail pair who first introduced their babies to his seed. This Five-Acre Farm mostly "farmed" birds, and there was no monetary profit in that, but there was "healing of the heart" and "flighty entertainment" such as that provided by feathered "friends."

Summer gave many opportunities for comfort: ample food, easy moonlit warm nights, sunny days, and play, play, play. Some wild creatures have summer responsibilities. Birds are an example of this responsibility. This is their time to nest and raise their young.

Mama Robin was doing all the right things at the Farm, but her result was not good. It was a wet morning when this Mama Robin sat on the fence, silent and cold, with drenched wings drooping from heavy rain the night before–very much a demeanor of sadness and confusion. She had been so busy before with finding her mate, building a nest, laying her small blue eggs, and then warming them until her featherless babies hatched.

After that, she had worked steadily, warming, protecting, and feeding those babies. She often hopped across the grassy yard listening for worms, cocked her head with ear to the ground followed by a quick attack with her beak. Then with worm held tightly, she leaned backward for a stronger pull while the limber-bodied worm wiggled and fought to stay in the soil. After winning the tug-of-war, Mama Robin beat the worm on the ground. Then she broke it into smaller pieces, so she could gather it in her beak and carry it to her babies in the willow tree above. Mama Robin did not even notice she was being observed while doing her repeated mama job. Grandma watched her often and wondered, *Is that bird thinking? Is she planning? Three babies, so I need three little pieces for three little mouths*? She did fly up into the tree with those pieces of worm in her beak.

"Naaa, birds can't count!" Grandma often turned her thoughts into spoken words, talking to herself. Grandpa probably would not hear her and, even if he did hear, he was used to her mumbling. She knew that and often consulted herself, knowing she would get an answer she would like. (It should be noted here that Grandpa believed Daddy Robin also fed their babies. Maybe that is true also.)

This rainy morning Mama Robin just sat on the fence motionless. She looked much like a human mother who has lost a child. The mama bird really had lost her babies. A few days prior, a hawk had swooped through the yard and was chased out over the fence with a tiny body held in its claws. Magpies flew after it pecking and squawking, while the hawk took its prey up and away over the trees. Perhaps the hawk had a Magpie baby but, since Magpie nests were not built over the yard, probably the prey was a tiny Baby Robin. The baby had undoubtedly fallen from the high nest, which had been built on a limb above where the sad mother bird was sitting in the rain. Mama Robin had often taken worms to that high nest.

No! Magpies are not sweet protective guards. In fact, they are a gang more than happy to raid another bird's nest. The day prior to Mama Robin's sad morning, a black and white long-tailed gang of Magpies had attacked another defenseless baby, a little Robin which had landed on the grass of the front yard. Its little body had not grown strong enough to fly away from their attack, so it was violently beaten by the squawking gang.

Two adult Robins made futile cries and efforts to defend their baby, but the flogging continued until Grandpa finally, from inside the house, heard loud bird cries and intervened. But by then the baby was dead. What could Mama Robin do on this rainy day, after her babies were both gone? She seemed not to know as she perched slumped, dejected, and lonely. Was that rain or tears in her eyes? Even an easy worm was only worth one nibble and she threw it aside—not hungry and with no babies to feed.

It was easy for Grandma to see defeat in the little bird's eyes, as it sat dejected on the board fence. *Will she have the strength and courage to start over?* Grandma saw the little bird's sadness and wondered how she could endure the loss of human babies if she was in the same situation.

Robins are known to have two summer broods. "So, will she try again?" Grandma thought aloud with empathy for the sweet mama's pain. Grandma was mentally bombarded with other questions about Mama Robin's future. *Will she use her same nest to lay and warm more delicate blue eggs which will then reveal pink featherless bodies? Will the same predators threaten her second family? ...But those predators exist anywhere she builds? Will Mama Robin be one of the strong ones? Will she have more babies to see a sunny tomorrow or will her broken heart cause her to fly away defeated by Mother Nature?*

Another bird mother who had often caught Grandma's eyes was the Mama Killdeer. When the Mitchells were first at the farm, often one of them nested on the low side of their land. There plants were sparse and rocks were plentiful, just what killdeer prefer. Often Mama Killdeer would see a creature, human or otherwise, approaching where her eggs were hidden among the rocks. She would try to cause the curious to follow her so they would not find her nest. While crying loudly and drooping one wing she would seem to limp the opposite direction to entice the invader away from her eggs or babies. Often that worked until humans got wise, then the wise humans hunted in the opposite direction of her ploy. However, a nest hunt rarely succeeded because the eggs looked so much like just small speckled rocks.

Grandma never did find Mama Killdeer's nest. Killdeer were not often seen at the farm in later years, so they must have found other places to nest. Perhaps killdeer left because large animals lived on the farm and big feet might have crushed her family which was nested on the ground. Or was it chemical sprays used on the weeds which made her nest unusable?

Grandma did once see a Killdeer suffering in a field which had been newly dampened with weed spray. It appeared from the bird's actions it was dying. That suggests that anything in or near its nest would also be in danger. Maybe that is why so few of those little birds are seen in nature in recent years.

Also, current farming techniques would damage the habitat in which Killdeer live and nest. Rock patches are tilled and adapted to produce crops, not to produce little birds. Green fields are nice but they do not make homes for Killdeer.

Predators, like cats, would find Killdeer as an easy prey because that bird's life is mostly spent on the ground. Though baby Killdeers' long legs carry them soon and fast, they are still down where predators lurk. Most predators would be able to smell their presence, unless they are like some other babies which have no scent. The adults can fly quickly when danger cannot be distracted away, but their imitated injury often works to distract any creature which approaches their nest. Also, the loud plaintive penetrating cry they make creates such chaos the attack may seem futile and deter the hunter.

At best a Killdeer's life is not easy.

Chp. 11: "Dark Nights"

Often, in the dark of night, Fuzzy Butt made noisy demands to go outside to relieve himself. That meant he had to be accompanied by a protector, since he was old and fragile and cougars were known to kill dogs, which was something occurring frequently in the area. That protector was Grandma. At age seventeen, Fuzzy Butt could not even manage the front steps and, being deaf and somewhat blind, he would be unaware of a possible attack until it occurred. So, regardless of darkness and her fear of possibilities, Grandma was always there to serve him with a can of pepper spray in her hand and her thumb on the trigger.

On one such trip outside into the dreadful darkness the resident stray named Kitty climbed to the front stoop and stretched her neck with head high, while staring into that darkness. Then she streaked away toward the back of the house. Since cats can see well in the dark, Grandma knew there was something to be feared lurking nearby in that shadowy place. Quickly Grandma grabbed Fuzzy Butt and headed for inside the house.

Regardless of Grandma's fear, the outside "potty calls" continued, often several times a night. There was no other way to deal with Fuzzy Butt's need. Cautiously, Grandma turned on many lights and even watched the roof to make sure a cougar was not lurking there. She was as watchful as a wild animal, though she was not equipped with more powerful senses like that of wild animals. She had no choice except to face the nightly ordeals, handicapped by being human. (Yes, an acquaintance had experienced a cougar on his roof. It was looking down at him. Trees in the yard had provided it a way up onto their roof… and Grandma and Grandpa had several big trees on all sides of their house!)

On one of those dark fear-filled nights, a bird somewhere in the top of the yard trees sounded out a raspy, "Scree! Scree! Scree!" Grandma consoled herself that it was probably just a little screech owl, using its night vision to hunt for exposed rodents. Maybe it was that tiny owl, but a little later there was a loud cat "Eooowww!" from the other side of the house. *Was that a cat fight or something more ominous--like the result of a hungry big bird attacking and packing away a stray kitten?* Grandma believed she had heard that kitten sound when they first came to live at the Five-Acre Farm but, by the time a cry is heard, there is no action that can be done to help. It was both fear and memories which made Grandma shiver.

Grandma knew some owls fly without making any sound from their wings, so they could easily catch unwary prey. She had to stay near Fuzzy Butt, while hoping the squall was only Miss Kitty in a loud conversation with another stray about rights to be in the yard.

There often were strays which came to the Five-Acre Farm where they found safety in the barn. It seemed the road provided for an easy dropping site to leave unwanted animals. That may have been the reason a single duck came wandering down that road and made a right turn into the Mitchells' house lane. When strays are dropped, it is impossible to know where they came from. The lost animals just find safety where they can, and the farm must seem safe. The cover of night often serves as the time for dropping the unwanted. They just show up the next morning as very lonesome strays.

Once there was a little white pup seen on a winter morning, acting frantic because of logging trucks roaring past it on the road in front of the Five-Acre Farm. Those large trucks were headed to the mountains to get their loads and they were traveling fast. Little pup seemed to be dodging or running with them, until it finally decided to leave the road to hunt a safer place to hide. It raced toward the barn, though its tiny tummy on short legs seemed to be dragging through the snow. It could not get in through the same crawl-space cats would find, but Grandma saw it there at the barn and went to rescue it.

Early that morning Grandpa had seen a car at the corner where three different roads intersect. That car was parked there and a man and boy were outside of it. A reason for them to be standing there, was the possibility that the little pup may have just been dropped there. That will never be known as a fact, but it was a very real possibility. Why else would they just be standing there looking down the road?

The little pup could have brought complications at the Five-Acre Farm and its actions made them fear for it. Its willingness to be on the road meant it might be killed on that road where it was first seen. It was very lively and hard to control, but it would be a sweet pet if it was placed in the right home, and the Five-Acre Farm was not the right home.

The baby dog was taken care of for a short time and then it was advertised to find it a home. It was a little female. Grandma named her "Baby." She was accepted by a young woman, but later the pup was again listed as needing a home. Baby took Grandma's heart, but only so many strays can fit into a home. Grandma does remember paying to have her spayed for her owner, and then being able to see Baby at the veterinarian's office. While Baby was still lying on her side, drowsy from the procedure, she looked at Grandma and wagged her tail; then she sniffed Grandma's hand as if she remembered. Grandma knew she could do nothing more for Baby and with a sad heart left while praying for that sweet white dog…a prayer for somebody to love her and give her a good home. Grandma will never know the rest of little white Baby's life story. She was a good dog and deserved a good family. All animals need kind human consideration, even deer.

Grandma worried about safety for Twin Mama and her babies. This was the deer family with Big-un and Little-un as fawns. They often bedded down in the Farm's bushes behind the barn because of Little-un's damaged hoof. They had many enemies to fear. Coyotes might attack as a pack to bring down even a grown deer. Bloody snow in an adjoining acreage revealed what was probably just such a kill, and then that snow melted the evidence away. Coyotes, those which were heard yodeling in the night by a nearby neighbor, had given clues regarding which predator had downed some kind of prey. A bloody trail revealed the prey had then been dragged into the bushes beside a little creek. The kind of predator and prey will remain uncertain, but that little creek is the same one flowing behind the Mitchells' barn.

**Guard inside,
Looking outside.**

On another of those dark scary nights, while Fuzzy Butt was circling in the yard, Grandma heard a coyote family talking by "yips, barks, and yodels." Their sounds easily carried through the crisp air. Coyote calls always sound like there are many in the group, but coyote vocalizations can be deceptive to the human ear, even in determining their location and number. Regardless, that meant Twin Mama and her babies might, on that very night, pay the ultimate price for being wild. If attacked she would try to fight, but to fight a pack would be futile and her littlest injured baby surely could not outrun a hungry aggressive coyote pack. A flashlight held by Grandma did not reveal reflective eyes, but the sounds probably came from an adjoining five-acre property. Again, Grandma rushed Fuzzy Butt inside, but she worried about the deer family. *Will Twin Mama and her fawns survive the night?*

The next morning, as her first act of the day, Grandma quickly asked Grandpa, "Have you seen the deer this morning?"

"Yeah, they're down in the brush lying down," Grandpa responded. Sure enough, there were two sets of small ears and one set of big ears showing above tall grass, as if listening for house action. They seemed comfortable, so there must not have been any night problems.

But what about tomorrow night?

Grandma remembers many dark nights in the depth of winter when their little old dog, Trapper (aka Fuzzy Butt), would have to make even more frequent trips outside. Grandma doubted that it was an actual need, but perhaps just restlessness because his old body had much pain. She would willingly take him outside, even if all he did was just stand there looking around at the darkness. Old age had dimmed his senses, so it would be impossible to trust he knew what was near, and whether it was friend or foe.

Since the temperature was low and the snow was deep, Trapper had to be wrapped in a doggie sweater. Then he had to have something warm put over his head, so his little ears would not freeze in the frigid night air. That protection was not easy when done several times a night but, because Grandma knew they would not have Trapper long, she remained patient and tried to fill his needs. The Mitchells both loved their little dog and dreaded the thought of losing him.

The little dog was so weak he could not go up or down the front steps, so he had to be packed to go both inside and outside of the house. He was not stable and could not see and could not hear. Trapper sometimes, during those hard older years of his life, would fall sideways in deep snow and not be able to get back up without a lift. The Mitchells would even sweep trails through the snow for him to travel for his potty business. But his age confusion often sent him off the trail resulting in him being stranded in the not yet shoveled deep snow. Grandma also had to be dressed warm while outside, so she could be there to retrieve him and place him back on the cleared paths when he strayed from them and seemed to be pleading for help.

Those were hard nights. They were hard because of the physical challenges for the little pet, but also hard because of the human emotional sadness caused by seeing their beloved pet suffering so very much.

Thinking back to nights in October when Trapper was a little more agile there was a Halloween night outside. October 31! Yes, Halloween, but "Trick-or-Treaters" rarely came to the Five-Acre Farm, because it was too far away from town and on dark roads with widely spaced houses. So, that evening was just like all others, calm and uneventful…that is, until the next early morning (referring to "end-of-the-night-kind" of early morning.)

At about three o'clock a.m. Fuzzy Butt had Grandma in the front yard darkness again. She was nervous, cold, and irritated with his multiple demands. Then a loud "Bang" was heard. Surely, it was from a large rifle that had been fired nearby–not firecrackers. *It must be a Halloween party gone sour or a jealous spouse discovering "an unwelcome guest,"* Grandma thought with a bit of humor. She knew that the next home toward town often had long night parties. Tents, bright lights, and loud music often accompanied their "events." But there never was shooting!

Grandma really did not want to know about such things … *much easier to remain unaware*, she thought. Then a second loud discharge was heard and she rushed toward her back yard, to the direction from which the gun sounds had come. The action was at the house just down the road toward town, the party property. That property was a short distance south of the Mitchell farm house where its field even shared a fence line.

Bright lights were shining outside and inside that house. Much action was occurring. A truck, equally lit up, seemed parked in the back yard shining its lights directly onto the house. A lady was loudly shouting in an excited voice. Her words, as if from outside, carried easily to Grandma's ears but were not distinguishable. The truck seemed to "rev" and move toward the house, but then it paused briefly and finally backed up and pulled out of their yard. It slowly drove onto the road which might bring it past or toward the Mitchell farm.

Grandma grabbed Fuzzy Butt and headed inside, not wanting to have it known that she had seen and heard the loud commotion. What if a person has been killed and now is to be dumped out in the mountains? Grandma's mind always seemed to imagine wildly! She feared, *Quick, tell Grandpa… he needs to know if something horrible is going on!*

She did not want to wake Grandpa but, feeling this could be a very serious problem, she believed he needed to be a witness also. Admittedly she tended to exaggerate problems, but this was a very unusual event to be happening so late at night … and on Halloween! She scurried to his bedside and started shaking his bed.

By the time she got Grandpa awake there was nothing wildly unusual happening there--no outside lights, no truck, nobody yelling, just nervous people inside that well-lit house rushing repeatedly back and forth in front of a window. But it was after three o'clock in the morning! No more cars drove away as if escaping a violent situation. Well, one car did leave but it seemed to be calmly headed toward town, and there was still a person moving around inside the house. Nothing impressed Grandpa as a possible problem from what he saw, so he went back to bed and quickly went to sleep again.

Grandma tried to imagine some scenario which would explain the events of the evening. She also shivered and the hair stood up on her arms from both cold and fear, but she knew there would still be many nights alone in their yard, extremely watchful nights! And what about those neighbors who celebrated so greatly for things like full moons and Halloween?

If a human has been shot the newspaper will tell us tomorrow, Grandma comforted herself hoping to forget all that had occurred. Then with no other alternatives, Grandma tried to go to sleep, and finally did with Fuzzy Butt nested on the floor beside her.

The story about the Halloween shooting was never reported in any newspaper, so Grandma had to make other assumptions about what might have happened. *A stray dog wandered around the neighbor's kennel? A deer was shot...nahhhh, the truck would not have headed to the mountains with an animal shot for food. So perhaps it was another animal to be disposed of... a cougar ... a cougar drawn to their kennel of dogs and seen near their house. A cougar about 600 yards away from our yard when Fuzzy Butt and I were outside!* And Grandma shivered again, thinking how fast cougars can run.

Nothing was ever publicly known about that mysteriously weird dark night in the Mitchells' neighborhood. All seemed simply peaceful "in Grandma's world," but there was no way to know what it was like at the house where the Halloween Night events had occurred. The family living there was young and not inclined to have elderly friends, so there would be no opportunity for Grandma to ask what had happened there on that mysterious night. Grandma could not get the thought of a cougar loose and prowling at three o'clock in the morning when she and Trapper were strolling in the yard.

With the rock wall just north of the Mitchells' farm, wildlife, including cougars, often passed through their small acreage. The wall did hold those ice caves which are deep cool caverns containing large hunks of rock and empty holes into the earth. Grandma had seen the caves, but she had never experienced their depth. It must have been a good place for a female cougar to birth or hide her babies away from threats of nature and from mankind. Significant is the fact that the rock wall which held the caves was known to contain cougars.

That rock cliff face was tall and bounded by large pine trees which often groaned when the wind blew. The face of solid rock must have held crevices which made homes for rattlesnakes, because they did show up at farms below. The large cliff was an interesting view when looking to the north from the farm, but it was not a friendly place to visit. Deer drank at the spring there and browsed at its protective bushes. On the wall's western side were the ice caves where the mother cougar had once hidden her babies.

If cougars used those caves once, there is great possibility they would use them again, and maybe even exit it to prowl the valley below, after dark!

If there was a cougar loose in the neighborhood, the only way to solve the problem would be to use a gun. Then the animal could be disposed of in the mountains. Is that what they did?

Is it possible there was a cougar loose when Grandma and Fuzzy Butt were standing in the dark yard for his night "potty business?" ... Possibly a cougar was there just the distance of one small field away! The thought made Grandma shiver again!

Chp. 12: "Fall"

"Go hide now! Go hide now!" the Quail lookout loudly announced while the flock had peacefully been working the ground for bugs, seeds, or whatever was edible. The lookout warned just in time before a Bird Hawk swooped in to capture its prey, nearly hitting the house. It missed both the house and Quail, but then it perched in the apple tree, waiting for the little birds to relax their guard. The hawk often found an unwise young one and carried it off to another place for its feast, leaving a mass of feathers to show where the bird's life had ended. ("Go hide now! Go hide now!" would be the sound rhythm of the Quail warning but, of course, Grandma did not really know the guard Quail's words. She pretended she did understand Quail talk because bird behaviors, if watched closely, "speak" almost as clearly as human words.)

A flock of twenty or more Quail often gleaned from the field while their guard, which was usually a rooster but sometimes a hen, perched high to watch for predators. Later in the season their main source of food was the seeds tossed by Grandpa onto the ground or into the large feeding tray. (Webster Dictionary describes a covey as "a pair of birds with a brood of young: a small flock." So, a flock can be more than one covey.)

Through summer the Quail hatched their hidden coveys eating as nature provided. Then later in the summer, when they started introducing their young families to the wider world, those large families (multiple coveys) made their reappearance at the Five-Acre Farm, sometimes exceeding fifty birds. Quail babies also had lessons in life to learn; one of those lessons was that a hawk cannot get them if they are hidden by brush of some sort. The lilac bush in the yard served that purpose well, and that is where they sometimes found shelter to avoid the hawk's attack. They were not always lucky.

One of their most unlucky times, though, was when crossing the road between the hill and the farm. Grandma and Grandpa came home once to see the road scattered with Quail feathers. Obviouly a vehicle had speeded through the little flock as they were trailing across the road. Grandpa's emotional attachment to the little birds, which he had been feeding, made that a very sad moment.

Sometimes, the Quail flock looked like many gray rocks of similar size scattered across the field until they moved. Then their tiny legs quickly propelled them while their funny little feather topknots saluted from heads of both roosters and hens. The males were bigger and more ostentatious, with a black "mask-like" design on their faces which the hen did not have. The responsible male (or female) lookout guard was usually perched high, while steadily watching for a threat, even if it meant his job kept him from eating. When the little flock moved away, the rooster would quickly hop from his oversight perch, then grab a few meager bites before he rushed to follow the others to again be their guard.

**Quail families stayed near
during summer and winter.
Their count was sometimes fifty or more.**

Miss Kitty, the resident stray, often stalked Quail. She was a good hunter and those little birds appeared to her like they would be an easy meal. As the little brown "humps" moved slowly, while feeding across grass in the bottom field, they seemed to be ignoring Miss Kitty, but they were watching her. Each time she moved sneakily toward them the little gray feathered birds simply fed further away. Then impatient Kitty made an all-out attack by springing forward and up with her claws extended. She grabbed only air!

The Quail had flown just high enough so a cat could not reach them. The birds had outwitted and outmaneuvered Miss Kitty. Dejected she turned and went back to the house pouting. At least it looked like pouting to Grandma after the little birds flew right over Kitty's head in their escape.

Grandma realized that same scenario probably occurred between cougars and turkeys, except both predator and prey were much larger and much faster.

There was one time when Miss Kitty proudly came down the lane with a feather-filled mouth. Grandma raced toward her scolding loudly, causing the startled Kitty to open her mouth in surprise as she dodged Grandma's flailing hands. The little Quail flew away, right out of Kitty's mouth and over Grandma's head. Grandma's smile reflected her thoughts, *Boy, did little Quail have a story to tell that night at the Quail table!*

Swallows bunked in the birdhouses at the farm, but they only spent summers there, unlike the constant Quail guests. Two or more birdhouses were provided, but Swallows must not have shared locations well because only a couple houses were ever used each year. Swallows were choosy about which birdhouse to use. One with a lower roof was never claimed, though it sat high on the loading chute where a landing spot was easily found above the chute. On another the opening was too large, allowing other birds to reach inside. Two houses must have been too close together, because only one house ever gained a family. Also, yellow-jackets were a problem, because they built their nests inside and were not friendly roommates. The Mitchells did not make life easy for the Swallow families, but they tried to help by fighting yellow-jackets and cleaning birdhouses.

It was both a male and female Swallow which raised their family. After the babies hatched there was much action in and out of the little round opening and then even chirping sounds came from inside as the parents arrived with food. It appeared both the mother and father delivered food to them and often one parent would sit on the roof waiting for the return of the other. The adult birds were kept very busy because they usually had more than one baby.

Both parent birds even helped teach the babies to fly. It was an absolute celebration when a baby took flight and the parents flew circles with it. Swoops, dives, circles, and happy chirping filled the air as the family all flew and cheered the baby on, until it returned to land on their roof. Over-and-over-again, they circled as both flight and landing seemed practice and celebration.

At a later time in summer many Swallows would collect and sit on electric lines together or fly in large groups around and around as if gathering their young ones for a long flight to a warmer southern location.

After they abandoned their birdhouse, they did not come back again until the next year. It would be impossible to know if the Swallows which returned the next spring were the same ones which used it the year before. All Grandma and Grandpa knew was that after the weather got mild again a pair (or more) of those little purple birds would come to their birdhouse and appear to be trying to decide if it would work for their summer home. The birds seemed to be checking all the possibilities before making their decision. With toes clinging to the edge of the hole their little heads would peer inside and then they would fly away, or return to look again. The decision must have been hard because never did they just enter and stay. Instead, humans only knew they had chosen after they were discovered nesting there sneakily. Then, if they were returning after their winter away, their summer job started over again to end in the fall when they "packed up" and again left.

$$*****$$

While fall leaves fell and winds started puffing their cheeks while scattering loose leaves to-and-fro, Twin Mama and her babies were often seen in the corral and barn brush where apples were still dropping as gifts from above. *Bless that old apple tree.*

Little-un sometimes looked like her hoof was getting straight, but at other times if she put her weight on it, the damaged hard part flopped loosely toward the outside seeming barely attached. The old couple was leaving the problem to Mother Nature, but Grandma thought maybe it would help to pray to Father God. It seemed possible to Grandma that Mother Nature and Father God "walked hand in hand." So, she prayed and watched for healing while Twin Mama took thoughtful care of her two babies, and sometimes even that extra fawn. Twin Mama knew what her injured little one needed, so she was providing that as best she could. Did she know her little one could not manage getting through a fence? Would she provide defense if an enemy approached her young family? Yes, undoubtedly, she would. One day Grandma even saw that motherly defense.

The young twins were in the corral eating apples and a small doe came to join them beneath the tree. Twin Mama rushed at the little doe with teeth bared, body low, and head aimed straight as an arrow for that unwelcome intruder. Twin Mama's mind and actions clearly implied, ***My children need these apples! Go find your own***! She meant to drive the intruder away and the young doe understood that aggressive attack and immediately left. Then Twin Mama ate apples while guarding from outside the corral. Only her fawns feasted inside their Garden of Eden.

While observing that confrontation Grandma thought, *The young doe who yielded so quickly, though she was really doing nothing wrong, is probably Timid. Timid never fights back!* (Timid is first found in Chp. 8, pg. 41, paragraph 2; pg. 42.)

Now and then other lone fawns were seen near Twin Mama, who welcomed their presence. Grandma wondered where the adults were and verbalized her curiosity, "Are they all orphans or have they just run away for a bit?*"*

Grandpa said, as he noted Twin Mama's family still around, "I'm surprised that injured fawn has lived so long." Grandpa's voice revealed concern showing he had a tender heart. Grandpa had familiarity and acceptance of Mother Nature's ways, but when observing the little fawn he said, "Good! It's still alive. I was afraid it'd die." Grandma just kept hoping and praying for a miracle as she studied the injured Little-un.

Though Grandpa emoted an exterior "tough as a horny toad," everybody knew about his "tender underbelly." Grandpa's gentleness showed especially in the way he cared for Fuzzy Butt, their little white friend. The little dog had a reserved spot on the armrest between the front car seats. Each morning, before the pet got too old, the little friend sat there to go to town with Grandpa for that "coffee and gab" at the local service station. Each morning when they traveled, Fuzzy Butt barked and cleared the road of all wandering dogs--at least he thought he did. But, after the little pet got old, Grandpa packed him to the car's back seat where his pet slept for most of their "morning event." The bond of love between them was strong, an affection which years would never break for Grandpa.

One day in the past (even before Mama Deer, Delawna, and Twin Mama's time of birthing on the farm), when Grandpa was driving on another road around the hill, he paused for a small herd of deer crossing in front of his car. He did not rush them, but the last baby was so fearful it quickly jumped over the fence where it should not have tried. The wire trapped it. Frantically it kicked and wiggled but was unable to escape, so Grandpa went to rescue it. While pushing the wire down, Grandpa lifted the fawn's legs up and finally got both hind legs untangled from the wire. Quickly the little one raced from its predicament to catch up with the other deer who were then out of sight in the trees across the road. Without Grandpa's help the wires probably would have been a death sentence for that little fawn.

Another time, the Mitchells and a couple of friends were traveling down a road through a herd of elk to view the herd's young calves. A surprised Grandpa pointed down toward the borrow pit beside the road and stammered, "There's one…it's hung…in the fence! Hear it crying? …down there!"

An elk calf, which was nearly hidden by tall grass, was tangled between wires of the fence beside the road. The car stopped, and Grandpa went to the little elk's rescue even before Grandma did, but both knew the calf would die if left there. Its bleating cries rang out while its wild-eyed mother watched nervously. The other cows gathered behind her in curiosity and fear, while some simply fled.

The cow elk, assumed to be the mother of the trapped calf, stood at the far side of the road with her head held high, her nose flared, and ears alert waiting for her calf, and most certainly deciding whether to attack those humans hovering over her bleating baby. Meanwhile Grandpa was on his knees in the grass and rocks at the roadside, trying to release the calf. Grandpa manipulated the tangled wires and a little leg, while Grandma held the top wire high trying to release the barb which had penetrated deeply into the calf's belly skin. Finally, release was accomplished and the baby kicked backward then frantically raced away. However, it was so frightened it raced in a half-circle then charged head-first back through the fence, making the wires rattle but not break. Somehow, the frightened little calf was able to get through the wires and dashed straight to its mother. Did it have cuts? Maybe. Humans had no way of knowing about that.

That same day, when driving further out into the mountains, Grandma and Grandpa had seen a calf elk trapped where it had tried jumping over a wire fence, but its back toes caught on the top wires. Its hind legs were then hung behind the wires which held it suspended at the groin. Finally, it somehow wiggled loose and slowly limped toward the herd. Wire can cut, and wire can tear, and wire can break body parts! The humans did not know what the calf's injury was, but it most certainly had been damaged. While remembering that scene Grandma wondered, *Was that situation the same as what had happened to the little fawn, to Little-un? Had her hoof become torn by a wire?*

Had Little-un, been in a jump across a fence and found herself trapped by the wires? Without help, she might have struggled until flesh and bone tore, thus releasing her. Of course, there were many situations which might have caused the little deer's injury. It might have been a steel animal trap set for cougars, bobcats, or coyotes on the hill. Grandma knew a trapper who did trap in that area for money, but his traps had no way of "knowing" which kind of animal to catch. In one known instance, a farm pup was found trapped and luckily was released by a hiking neighbor. That occurred in the same vicinity Little-un might have traveled before she was injured.

There were many possibilities which could inflict a hoof injury. A little deer hoof could have triggered a trap and, by the fawn's struggle to extricate itself, the hoof was torn loose. Maybe the sharp metal jaw of a trap cut the hoof. Maybe, while running, the fawn stepped on something and was injured. Maybe a car had hit Little-un, since the littlest animals were often the ones last to cross a road. Cars did race down the straight road between the Five-Acre Farm and the hill. There were so many "maybes."

Grandma had a theory that bottom fence wires should be higher, so animal babies can crawl under them instead of trying that dangerous jump over the top or getting trapped while trying to wiggle between the wires. Grandma often wondered what God thought about mankind carving up His beautiful Earth into little sections bound by fences–fences which held domestic animals, but which also hurt the innocent wild ones. Surely that was not part of God's plan.

If fences are built to keep domestic cows and calves in a pasture, then higher bottom wires would benefit the cattlemen as well. Their little calves sometimes get on the opposite side of the fence from their mother cow and cannot find how to get back to her. If the bottom wire was higher, then all babies could get back to their mother more easily. That higher bottom wire would not allow the cow to shift pastures, but it might save the lives of some babies. Isn't this just logical?

Cows become frantic when their calves cannot get to them, but there is not a thing they can do to get through the fence either. That can have a tragic end!

And, yes, this fence trap effects wildlife as well as domesticated animals. Close observation while driving through areas where wild animals live and fences encircle those pastures, will prove without a doubt that fences cause death among baby animals. Even Grandma and Grandpa experienced seeing that and were able to release at least three living babies. However, other rural trips revealed babies which had died while tangled in wire fences. That is a sight nobody would like to see.

Chp. 13: "Visitors"

Many signs preceded the beginning of winter. One sign was the celebration of Thanksgiving when the Mitchells' younger family came home for dinner and a "sleep-over." Their Grandies had grown into their teen years; one had even gone away to college. For Grandma and Grandpa each year with their children and grandchildren had its own special kind of sweetness. But these older years were bittersweet because, like the deer, the young humans tend to "migrate with their families." That shifting of homes often causes holidays to be held without those precious offspring present. It is a sign the young ones are making good full lives for themselves, and the older ones would only choose to have that be true. But it does make lonely moments for those left behind. Time changes many things.

Before Thanksgiving, Twin Mama had taken her family away, just as she had done before Little-un was injured. Grandma mentally contemplated. *Did that mean Little-un was healed or did it mean a predator ended the problem while at the same time causing the others to flee?* Deer lives were mostly a mystery to the older couple who only knew, with certainty, what they saw on their five acres.

One event the Mitchell couple saw was the flying arrival of a hungry flock of Starlings. Those birds may have been the reason for Twin Mama taking her family away from the farm. The Starlings found the remaining apples that were still hanging on the limbs of the old apple tree. It took only one day for the large number of Starlings to eat or knock down most of those remaining apples. The next day, a turkey migration found the fallen apples and cleaned the ground. Some of those large turkeys even flew up onto those fragile limbs and knocked more apples down. The turkeys had a huge feast. After those raids, there were no more apples for deer in their Garden of Eden -- no more apples for Twin Mama's family. That occurred in the fall, with winter soon on its way.

After the snow came, Grandpa had to shovel it aside just to make a bare spot of ground to toss his birdseed where it would not be buried in white. Then his intended guests had to get there quickly before the snow again covered their food. The Quail would not eat beneath a sheltered spot, perhaps because it felt like a trap to them. Grampa had tried to make a snow-blocking cover over the spot where he threw the seeds, but Quail would not go underneath any covering. So, to meet their needs, Grandpa shoveled snow, then tossed birdseed. With that done, many "ground feeders" came. This task sometimes happened twice each day, depending upon the amount of snowfall. Sometimes even feeding spaces were cleared by using "Poppin' Johnny" caterpillar with its blade down. Those trail spaces benefitted birds, deer, pets, and even humans who were walking to the barn.

About then, various little snowbirds and Quail showed up in great numbers at Grandpa's feeding spots. The small black-headed Juncos came yearly, but only in winters, to join the ground-feeding Quail, Sparrows, Doves, and Magpies. (Webster dictionary calls Juncos *"any of the genus Junco... small widely distributed American finches, usually having a pink bill, ashy gray head and back, and conspicuous white lateral tail feathers."*) Most of the little birds, except the Magpies, Quail, Chickadees and Sparrows, were there for fall only. Though others migrated through, the faithful ones stayed all year long, somehow adapting to the cold. Then when the cold weather got even colder, bird numbers would become nearly overwhelming. (Webster dictionary does not use capitals for bird names, but Grandma believes all names should be capitalized out of respect, even nicknames. She has a great fondness for names, so this book honors her wishes.)

The Quail families were large–must have included aunts, uncles, and cousins. Such a funny little parade they made, a follow-the-wise-leader line with topknots a-flopping. When the leader fell into a snow-hole and could not be seen, each consecutive topknot by turn dropped out of sight. Then one-by-one each would "pop up again" out of the hole. Funny, none thought to go around the hole! (The leader must have been their old "wise guide," one to never be questioned. There must be a hidden lesson in that for mankind. Perhaps something like, "Dare to be different!" or "Think for yourself!")

When the wind and snow were too brutal, Quail would make a little huddle, like a football team around their quarterback, with heads down toward the middle and rears out. In this way Quail feathers thickly covered the outside of the huddle while their heads in the middle were protected from the wind by other feathered bodies. If an outside Quail felt cold, it started pushing into the middle of the huddle. In doing this they alternated, each being heated while taking turns inside where it was warmer. Then, after being warmed, each would be pushed outward again by the colder ones who were pushing in. It was just a natural migration. When huddled like this beneath a bush they could withstand extreme storms.

The snow made it difficult for Miss Kitty to hunt, so she had to rely on kitchen scraps and bagged cat food. The snow was too deep for her to find mice. She could not move through the deep snow to catch birds without leaps; however, leaps are not a stalking motion but instead somewhat like a kangaroo sneaking up on a mouse. It did not work! Her black and orange calico hair, puffed and full for the winter, made her as obvious as a clown's nose. Little birds just flitted around through the snowy bushes avoiding her, while Miss Kitty waited only feet away with wistful eyes and drooled. The birds seemed to be tittering, *"We see you! You can't catch us! Ha Ha!"* She spent hours furtively hidden behind the trees near the birdseed, waiting and hoping for an unwise bird. That did not serve her well.

Snow made issues for Fuzzy Butt, too. How does a little dog "go pot" when belly-deep in snow? That meant a "potty spot" had to be swept daily, and sometimes hourly, just so he could move his short legs through the deep snow. Grandma kept a broom handy on the "front stoop" so circular trails could be swept before bringing the little white fellow outside to follow the trails around and back. Often, he just stood and inhaled the scents of nature, something he experienced less in wintertime. Grandma waited patiently, understanding his need, but also watching for danger. Danger did come even when the snow was deep. Deer visited often and one buck walked around the yard fenced looking in at "the dog" inside. Grandma is convinced it would have made an attack if she had not been there to scare it away.

＊＊＊＊＊＊

One snowy afternoon a group of Mule Deer arrived in the back field. There were maybe as many as three does and four fawns. Delawna was not there and, since she was absent, probably Dawna was still away, too. Were Little Buck and Big-un there? Possibly. None in the field had horns, but by this time of year does and bucks might have looked much alike, because bucks lose their antlers in wintertime. It is possible Adolescent and Handsome were there also.

One of the fawns was smaller and, if studied closely, it appeared to have a slight limp in a hind foot. Grandma puzzled, *Can that possibly be the injured Little-un?* Grandpa thought it was, but Grandma was just cautiously optimistic. "I want to believe that's Little-un," she told Grandpa. "But how did it get so much better? I wanted a miracle, and maybe I got one!" Among the other fawns there was a sturdy one, which might have been Big-un and a doe which could have been Twin Mama. This was their familiar grazing spot, their protected haven. *Why not believe Little-un is better? It is logical... but wears no guarantee!*

Grandma was trying to convince herself about the happy outcome. This certainly was a better result for Little-un than the other possibilities. *Yes, I will believe! I want the happy ending,* she thought with a smile.

That night on one of her trips outside with Fuzzy Butt she saw white mounds in the front field. That meant something was sleeping very near the lane, just beyond the shop, and somewhat close to the front of the house. She knew there was nothing for her to fear in those bodies beneath the snowy blankets. Likewise, they had nothing to fear from her, so the deer did not move all night. It was a peaceful feeling to have the deer family settled close, and to believe Little-un had somehow recovered.

That next morning, as Grandma awoke and pulled the curtain open to see if it had snowed more, there were still several white humps of snow beside the lane which led from the house to the road. They were not identifiable, as other than snow, until one hump moved and its big-eared deer head was raised. Usually that location was off-limits by the deer, but for some reason they chose to be close to the house that night, much closer than they usually dared to be.

Several of the herd stayed there sleeping until later that morning when Grandpa drove out of the lane to the main road and disturbed them. One which appeared to be a little buck stood and slowly awakened the others. There seemed no urgency for the others to be up and away. As it often did for the Mitchells, the deer felt like part of their family. Is it possible even the deer felt like part of the Mitchell family, too?

It gave Grandma a good feeling to see the many humps just beyond her bedroom window. For the humans, they were a good replacement to fill the absence caused by the old couple's own human family members, who were then missing for a variety of reasons. Certainly, the deer were not like real children, but instead they were just "something to love." They made a warm spot in old human hearts by their trust, though the weather was anything but warm.

**A visit from Handsome
on a cold winter day
before he lost his antlers.**

Grandma continued trying to recall, even years later, about those humps of white near the house. Did she really see horns buried beneath the snow? Her mind remembered just nice round humps, big snow humps and little ones. She had concluded, at the time of this story, that there were bucks in the mix of bodies after they had awakened. Bucks do lose their antlers in wintertime, and she did not remember any antler-like humps in the snow.

The picture of Handsome (on page 73) shows him looking across the yard fence and he was still wearing his antlers. There is clearly snow on the ground, so he had not yet shed his crown. This was photographed on a different day than the "snow humps" and it may have been taken earlier in the winter. Then he could have still had his antlers to shed later. The snow in the later event was much deeper and probably later in the winter, so it is still possible Handsome was there for the "humpy-snow party." But maybe he was there without his crowning antlers.

Another possibility considered, about the antlers not showing while blanketed by the snow, was that the antlers may have been rested onto the deer's shoulder while it was sleeping. Grandma could not recall seeing a sleeping buck to know the way they managed to sleep with those horned "heavy heads." Perhaps a clue might come from Chapter 15 which states, "hind legs were pulled under its body and its head was settled onto its shoulder." This refers to the head pointing downward while resting it gently on the same side shoulder.

Is that the position deer might take while sleeping, or perhaps while it is very cold? Is that the position in which a buck would typically sleep while holding his heavy rack in a manner that would relax neck muscles? Would that drop the antlers low enough so they would not make a conspicuous hump in the snow? Grandma could not answer any of these questions, but she still believed a buck was there blanketed with snow and he arose to greet the morning. That previous summer both Handsome and Adolescent would have grown antlers.

The sleeping deer were encircled by the Five-Acre Farm fence on three sides with the shop/ garage on the fourth side. Beyond the north fence was the road which typically held a lot of traffic, but not so during a blizzard such as the night they slept nearby. These fences and buildings formed a small enclosure with human presence on all sides. Did that closeness to the human residence mean they trusted humans? Did they want to be where human outside lights kept their night bright?

It seemed strange that deer would have chosen this close location as a safe place to settle for the night, unless they felt some protection by human presence. The road would not have been human protection, or danger either, because of the blizzard keeping away traffic. But this property had provided apples even when snow covered everything, because deer often found apples waiting on the cement backyard step. Grandma had even gleaned from the neighborhood trees to have a supply for just such use. Maybe the deer could feel affection for those humans who lived inside that house, where even in blizzards the nightlights often shined brightly.

Chp. 14: "Winter Survival Struggles"

Flights of Geese kept the sky noisy as they migrated south, often landing for a rest at the river or at the many ponds in the valley where the Mitchells lived. The Geese would not stay long in the valley, though, because the cold would eventually freeze their water sources. It was quite funny watching a Goose land on a pond and then discover the water was frozen hard-- "walkable not swimmable." The hard landing probably jolted it at first, then while puzzled the big bird squatted as if to paddle away. It took a short time for the heavy-bodied bird to realize it must walk instead of paddle to move forward.

Grandma and Grandpa often called their Five-Acre Farm "The Hell Hole" because of its winter hardships. In those hard times they stood looking out their windows into a blizzard so dense no neighborhood lights could be seen anywhere. Strong winds often blew the snow horizontally, and more than once the back door was covered outside, up to the top with snow. The door hole was a total white wall of snow when opened. The powerful winds roared through the pine trees on the hill, sounding as loud as a distant train, and drifts of blown snow were so deep even huge graders, which were used to clear the snow, could not push through. One night a driver parked the grader he had been using and walked out, because even that big piece of equipment was stuck.

The Mitchells were grateful when they still had electricity in such a storm. Sometimes electricity failed, making them miserable. That meant darkness, lack of heat, and with bathrooms that did not work because water had to be electrically pumped from their well. However, when seeing animals outside they realized their human struggles were small in comparison.

When winter settled in with full force, snow covered the ground heavily making it difficult or impossible for grazing animals to get food, especially when the snow had a frozen crust. Deer would strip bark from Buckbrush and even nibble on ornamentals in Grandma's flower garden. Deep snow caused deer and elk to be more vulnerable to predators because, when running through it, they lost their speed ability which helped them survive. Even birds struggled against the brutal winter weather and hunger. Imagine yourself as a bird trying to fly in a strong wind while searching for a safe shelter.

Quail families paraded across deep snow to eat Grandpa's bird seed at least once a day, but twice a day he delivered their seed feast inside and outside of the yard fence. Seed had to be sprinkled outside for those birds which could not get over or through the fence, but seed inside the fence was more vulnerable to other wildlife, like deer who can jump fences.

Drinking water for all wildlife sometimes froze solid; however, some springs flowed steadily, making at least a few small spots of open drinking water. That was the case at the Mitchell farm.

The Five-Acre Farm's freely flowing spring water came from the ground across the road. It usually had enough water to at least trickle down past the Mitchells' barn. There was no need for animals to seek water at the several nearby frozen ponds. Grandma was glad that was one hazard animals could avoid because, if they broke through the ice of a pond, they could possibly drown.

Many predators of small animals were often seen. Eagles were seen in flight. They and night predators could and would easily carry off prey the size of a cat. Kitten squalls were once heard at night as if it was being flown or dragged away captive of a hungry predator. That was the kind of night Grandma snuggled closer under her bedcovers, thankful for being human.

When the weather started getting more miserable, Grandma began taking trips with kitchen scraps down to the little shed attached to the open-front loafing shelter. The little shed was mostly used for storage, but it was an easy-access haven for stray cats or anything else small. Signs of use by strays convinced her food was needed there, especially in the winter, and it was usually eaten.

During summer, feral cats mostly fended for themselves by hunting rodents in the fields and buildings but, with snow on the ground, there would be many empty stomachs unless Grandma provided. It seemed a waste to simply dispose of food that might be relished by hungry cats, so Grandma daily made her trek through the snow to the little shed with left-over food scraps.

Grandma often entered the open-front shelter, but seldom entered the shed attached to it. The shed had no windows and she was not certain what creature she might meet in its dark interior. She simply slipped the food inside the door, or under the large gap beneath the door, and assumed food scent would attract the hungry. There were openings under the walls and door of that shed which had been dug by something other than humans. Through those holes small animals entered or even exited unseen when frightened. That is why Grandma never knew what might be inside the dark little building, so her fear caused her to avoid entering it.

On several snowy trips she observed tracks in the snow leading up to and inside the open-front shelter. They were not feral cat tracks, but appeared to be from a larger paw like a coyote or a neighborhood dog. There were also deer tracks. She knew a dog might scavenge the scraps, but she did not understand a deer's attraction to the open-front shelter.

Regardless, she continued bringing food while assuming her scraps were needed. Sometimes when she got there the paper dish, which had held the scraps, was pulled out through the hole under the door of the little attached shed. Usually, that container had been licked clean to the point of being shredded on the floor of the open-front shelter. That Grandma did not understand! That surely was not cat action. The containers had been mysteriously dragged from where Grandma had placed them just inside the door of the dark shed and remained out in the open-front shelter. She was puzzled, *What other animal would have liked human food scraps?*

For a while after the heavy snowfall, the deer seemed to stay on or near the Five-Acre Farm. During Grandma's night trips outside with Fuzzy Butt, her flashlight often showed deer eyes. The reflective brilliance of those eyes proved they were looking at her, too. They were usually seen between the house and the bushes.

The deer bedded after dark near the presence of people, but strangely there was one set of eyes showing separate from the cozy little group. That had Grandma puzzled. *Why would one deer be separated--ostracized? Could that be because it is an orphan? Won't they even let it sleep near them?*

There was an orphan in the group. Grandma was certain that was true, because one day she saw the fawn totally abandoned. That happened on one early morning after a night of heavy snow. There was a white snowy hump in the animal trail through those bushes behind the barn. She puzzled about what it was before she saw a lone fawn stand and shake off its thick white blanket of snow. Then it moved to join other deer, but there were none. Grandma could almost hear the fawn's frantic loneliness. ***Where are they? Where are they? What will I do? Where should I go?*** The lone fawn scanned through the bushes, looked distant for clues, paced back and forth to the corral, back to the barn, through the bushes, and even started to leave, but then changed its mind and returned to the familiar barn bushes.

In the middle of the little fawn's loneliness a flock of turkeys passed through the field. Fawn simply stepped back into protection of the bushes and watched the turkeys moving across the snow, quiet as ghosts past the fawn's brushy hiding place. The snow was crusted just enough so that sometimes the turkeys could walk on top of it. However, if one or both legs fell through the snow's icy hard surface, they had quite a struggle to pull their leg(s) back up to the frozen top. Theirs was a funny gait at best, a 1 and 2 rhythm, having a side-to-side body wobble with each step. Their long thin legs were their hope of survival, and to seriously injure one of those legs would be a death sentence. Without legs it could not travel with the flock to find food, water, or even get to their night roost trees.

It must have been painful to have their (four times two) bare toes constantly in snow and ice. Sometimes bloody marks were left on the snow, probably from icy shard cuts on their feet. Their movements were slow and measured and often they would stand on one foot and lift the other to tuck it into their warmer belly feathers, just resting for a short time. As a group they rested.

After all animals left, Grandma went to the barn and discovered bloody spots in the snow where turkeys had walked. Their snow injuries had bled. What a painful trip they had made traveling to find food and then returning to their roosts in those pine trees on the hill. The hungry flock often moved through the Mitchells' field, but rarely in the large number traveling together on that specific day. They had been trudging painfully on their way to more distant productive pickings, after they had gleaned what they could from the hill and lower brush patches.

The first turkeys there got the food and, with a flock that large, many did not have anything left to eat, so those slow ones got slower and weaker. This fitted Mother Nature's plan that only the strongest survive, because some would probably not survive a harsh winter and in this way that would strengthen the flock. With the cover of snow their food was meager and their bodies were beginning to show that. When needing a rest from the cold ordeal they would take a teepee-like posture, a three-point sleeping position.

**Flocks of turkeys
gleaned in the valley
during winter, but summered
on the forested hill and beyond.**

Two legs and the stiff tail supported a sleeping turkey, a tripod of sorts. Then, its head was pulled back into its scruff of neck feathers to warm the head's featherless red hide.

The mass of turkeys slept for a while in this manner, then shook snow off their feathers, popped their heads out of the protective covers, and walked again. (Chapter 3, pg. 15, is about turkeys in summertime, but wintertime flocks in the valley far exceed numbers of any summer valley visits.) In this time of cold when they did not do the proud mating dance, the male turkeys (called cocks, toms, or gobblers) still had an identifying feature which showed their gender. They had large wattles, flesh hanging down from their beak/head and one from the chest area. The turkey females (called hens) were less ornamented. (Read about the "snood and wattle" on page 15.)

In summertime, turkey flocks usually moved together but it was not the massive migration seen in fall or winter. It was always an interesting migration to watch with the toms easily recognized in their flock. The toms were more colorful, but all the turkey "garments" were precision in color, complete with "a white lacey trim" on the end of their tail feathers. They looked as if planned by a costume designer; their red heads were shaded with blue, their back feathers were bluish-brown, their tails had bands of alternating rusty brown and black with white narrow accents on their tails and wings. Altogether they made a colorful procession.

When turkeys were in flight, their tails would spread like many carefully decorated fans with rows of color ending in that narrow bright white scallop. Grandma knew because she once was beneath a flock's flight over her head. In the cold times, though, their manner was less ostentatious. In fact, Grandma did not see any of them fly in this winter group. They seemed to only be saving their energy to fly into their roost tree on the hill where the tall pines grew.

The fawn stayed hidden in the bushes until the turkeys were all gone. About three hours passed while the fawn was hiding and watching. After the turkeys left, the little deer continued pacing and looking in the distance, nervously hoping to see the herd. It was a lonely child abandoned by those it knew. A few times it started to leave the field and bushes as if to search further, but then would turn and come back to where it felt safest.

The herd, however, must not have valued the fawn or it would not have been left alone. Grandma felt certain its mother would not have left in such a way. That abandonment was even more proof this fawn was an orphan. Grandma was positive it was an orphan, probably the one not really welcomed in the deer's sleeping group, the one whose eyes had shown in the darkness separated from the others. She puzzled, *Is this orphan really Little Buck?*

The sleeping group had held about seven sets of eyes and, at other times there was seven with an added fawn. This was probably the same group in which the fawn would make eight. This may have been the same herd with the does Delawna and Twin Mama and their babies. So that might mean Orphan belonged to the group too, but Mama Deer was not there to protect or defend him. Mama Deer was not there to make sure her fawn was fed and welcomed to the group. It must have been Mama Deer which had fallen victim to the hunter, leaving her fawn as an orphan, the one which Grandma called Little Buck.

In the afternoon, when the other deer finally came back to the nearby field where there was a spring, the lonely fawn saw them. They were there to drink water, not to find him, but the nervous fawn raced to them, searching for familiar ones to connect with. He was so anxious to get to them he rapidly carelessly pushed between the fence wires which separated the two fields. The fawn was like a lost child crying, *"Mama, Mama,"* as it tore through wires and raced toward the others.

The little fawn was not hesitant in entering the herd and they did not act mean toward it. They just ignored it as it tried to mingle. Not even other small ones seemed to welcome it. However, it stuck like a "beggars' louse" (a sticky weed seed) into their herd as if trying to be certain to not be left again. It was trying to be "one of their family;" trying to be one of their herd. It needed them, regardless of being wanted or not.

The returning deer just nonchalantly allowed the lonely fawn in their presence. None greeted the fawn with any signs of recognition or affection, though the little one came right up to them. In fact, they may not have been the fawn's herd, but the lost one was obviously going to attach to them for deer companionship. Whether wanted or not it would become a part of the herd. It was not seen leaving with the herd, but for a time it was not seen at the farm. Nor was the herd seen at the farm.

Being a lone fawn is a dangerous situation and this baby must have sensed that. However, what it did not know was that there would be none among the herd to help as if it was one of their own. They had not treated the fawn as belonging to their herd since Mama Deer was killed. That was the way it was with adult deer...with most members of the herd anyway. Some does were an exception and they helped orphans, or at least easily accepted their presence.

This little fawn, through no fault of its own, was being rejected. The fault is in the human culture which does not understand the absolute need of baby animals for their mothers--all baby animals, even all human babies. Human babies' needs last much longer and, when they have a parent, their challenges are far less than those challenges faced by animal babies trying to survive alone "in the wild."

There are feelings, deep feelings, between mothers and babies, even animal babies, and they need each other. Grandma once saw a doe grieve the loss of her baby which had been killed by a car that morning. The doe kept watching the hill from the Five-Acre Farm as evening approached, but her fawn never came down from the hill that night or ever again. Her manner of constant watching clearly expressed sadness. She loved her baby! Babies love their mothers too, and it was for that reason this little fawn raced back to the herd. But there he found no mother!

Chp. 15: "A Hungry Visitor"

Grandma was convinced that this little lone fawn, which had been left sleeping in the snow, belonged to the herd of seven with which she had become so familiar. Grandma finally believed the orphan was Little Buck and most certainly he belonged to that herd, now eight. She officially claimed the orphan to be a male and the son of the missing Mama Deer. *It just must be Orphan. No more doubt. Now what do I call you? Little Buck or Orphan? You will be both to me!*

Later in the deepness of winter the little deer herd briefly visited the farm and then migrated away, looking to find better food sources. One young fawn mostly stayed on or near the farm, and was often seen around the barn and bushes. From this, Grandma concluded it must have been the orphan. Since it often hid in the birth bushes where Little Buck and Dawna were born, it seemed logical the lone fawn was seeking its familiar places of protection. Maybe he was drawn to the place where he had known his mother. Many of Grandma's observations further convinced her that Little Buck had truly lost his mother and was the orphan which rarely migrated with the herd. Mostly Grandma called him Orphan because he always seemed to be alone, even if there were other deer in the vicinity.

During the winter the deer were getting gaunt, though a neighbor for a time provided pellets for them in a long shallow trough in his field. That trough drew quite a deer crowd. It looked like all does and fawns, but could have been a mix because bucks were probably bald by then. Since the pellets were there during unusually warm sunny days many deer came and remained near the food while enjoying resting on the southern slope. It was a bareheaded mixture of contented deer lying on the sunny field, but orphans would not have been welcomed there.

(Encyclopedia World Book, copyright 1963, pg. 74 says, *"...deer shed their antlers each winter. The following spring, the buds of new ones appear. The buds soon grow into small, blunt antlers. Later, during the summer, they grow more and begin to develop branches called tines. A soft, velvety hair covers the antlers until they are full-grown. By autumn, the hair is shed, leaving the antlers tall and sharp. During the autumn mating season, rival males fight duels in which they push against each other's antlers until the weaker deer turns and runs away. Wisconsin Conservation Dept."*) Little Buck, had those hairy little nubbins when he was still just a baby.

Probably Orphan had found that food too, but the older deer would not have let him eat. There were no visual barriers between the Five-Acre Farm and the trough with many deer around it, but Orphan probably did not even try going there. Undoubtedly, he remained on the Five-Acre Farm, near the others, seeing them, but not getting food.

To join other deer in the neighbor's field was not a choice Orphan was allowed to make. If he had joined the deer at the trough, he would probably have been chased away soon. Surely, when they left the trough, there would not have been any pellets remaining for him to eat anyway.

One day Grandma saw the fawn jump the fence into the corral and chuckled to herself while thinking how messy he looked with his tail awry and his hair rumpled, like an unkept child. Turning to Grandpa she said with a smile on her face, "Looks like he has a bed-head…not a very tidy child." However, she thought he was surviving okay. It did not occur to her that his trips to the corral were to steal cat scraps. She did not realize those deer footprints into the three-walled shelter were his, and the food dug from under the shed door were his effort to get some of the cat scraps. She could not even imagine that deer eat human food scraps.

Orphan had to be very hungry to want table scraps, but that was probably all he could find to eat, if he got anything.

If she had only known what was really trying to get food, her actions would have been very different. Pellets for deer could have been left in that shelter and they would have been exactly what Orphan needed. But she did not know!

Now and then Grandma had put apples on the backyard steps for deer and the next morning there would be many hoofprints around the cement steps, but no apple pieces remained. Did the many hoofprints mean there had been many deer there? Maybe it was just one little hungry deer returning repeatedly with hope of finding apples.

Hay is said to damage deer so that seemed a poor alternative for feeding the lone fawn, and besides the other deer would not share hay anyway. Older more aggressive deer would have been there first, and young or timid ones would be chased away. Deer do not share well! Grandma thought that might be what happened to the apples at the step because she did know other deer often passed through during the nights. Orphan did not leave with them. He remained elusive either on or near their five acres.

Then there was one night when the temperature was far below zero and Fuzzy Butt needed to go outside at 3:30 that next morning. So, bundled in heavy clothes, Grandma took the sweater-wrapped little friend out into the crisp-cold blue dark night. Her steps squeaked in the frozen snow and her breath met the cold as a steamy mist. Moonlight and flashlight revealed one set of tracks from the birth bush to the cement step and back to the bush. The hungry Orphan had come for an apple and not even one was there. Because the single trail came from the birth bush, Orphan would have been the only deer to make that track.

Grandma had forgotten to put apples out that evening, but she vowed to do better the next night. Grandma then debated going to the cellar in the darkness to get apples to put on the step, but cold and cowardice kept her from going. Instead, she went back to bed. That was an act she would later regret!

**This is Orphan.
His eyes are asking for food
but Grandma does not understand.**

That night was even colder than the night before. Then at daylight Grandma saw many little hoofprints which had been made during darkness in the fresh snow. They were made by many fawn trips between the cement step and the birth bush. She knew hungry Orphan had just kept hoping, but there never was even one apple there. Hungry little Orphan was in so much need and Grandma had failed to give food. She was very sad and ashamed that she had been so selfish, just because of darkness and cold. Seeing those tracks she swore the next night Orphan would have a feast of apples waiting on that cement step. Grandma shivered remembering the boards and metal obstructions she had placed under the door to keep "dogs" from getting to the purchased cat food which the Mitchells also put there with the scraps. She remembered the large heavy sharp piece of metal she had wedged under the door to stop the digging which had made that hole larger. Her efforts did fill the hole and mostly stopped the digging. With hands holding her head she mumbled, "Oh! Why did I?" Grandma considered the horrible obstruction she had made because of believing she was stopping dogs. But it was not dogs that were needing her scraps!

But the next night did not come in the way planned. That very afternoon Grandma headed for the barn with many kitchen scraps. At the gate into the corral, which was always open, she noticed strange deer tracks in the snow. The tracks appeared to be from a small fawn also entering the corral. To get to the open-front shelter she had to go through that gate. The deer tracks were not sharp and clear, but seemed dragged with messy snow at their edges as if made by stumbling hooves.

"That is strange! The deer must have slipped on something," grandma told herself while stopping to study those tracks. Then Grandma went on toward the open loafing shelter with her scraps in her hands. But as she stepped into its wide open-front, she saw a little deer collapsed against the back wall. Its hind feet were tangled behind it and its head was upright arched over its back. Snow clung to its body, and even its eyelashes held a crust of crystalline white and were motionless as was the rest of its snow-covered body. Grandma was startled at the pitiful sight and felt like she was to blame. Words flooded from her, "You needed apples and I failed you. Oh, Orphan, I am so sorry! I am so selfish! You poor little one!"

Orphan remained motionless, so Grandma assumed it was dead and did not even approach it. That was a very cold winter day, colder than most, maybe minus 14 degrees or near that. Cold and hunger were thought to be the reason for the little deer's death and she knew she could have helped by solving at least one of those problems.

Grandma believed it was Orphan, and she rushed to the house in tears still believing the fawn was dead. Sobbing, she told Grandpa, "I think he's dead! Oh, I think he's dead!" She could not at this point even consider that it maybe was Little Buck.

After Grandpa understood what she was talking about, he shrugged and said, "There's nothing you can do now. If it's gone, it's gone!"

"But it just did make those messy tracks in the snow. It just got there!" Gramma half-sobbed.

Then, when describing to Grandpa what the little deer looked like inside the open shelter, she realized maybe it really was not dead. A dead deer's head would not be held upright in such a strange position, so it must still have life. Quickly she rushed to the barn again, but this time with apples, applesauce, oatmeal, and warm milk. With even a few old garments to help cover or dry the fawn, she knew each second counted. *If only I can get some food into it,* she thought.

The sadness inside Grandma seemed more penetrating than the icy air she breathed as she hurried back to the shelter with food and hopes that she could do something to help that weak baby.

She was grateful the little deer had sought a protected place, but the shelter was not a warm place. She wondered how often it had been in that shelter and if it really had been the fawn's hungry attempts to reach the cat food. *At least he will be dry and away from the snow,* she consoled herself.

Her thoughts raced for solutions, but she knew the increasing darkness of night was against anything she might plan. She did not have time to put a tarp over the shed's open front to stop the cold. There was no electricity to make it possible to bring in a heater. A fire inside the shed would be unwise and might catch all the outbuildings on fire. What could she do? Thoughts raced through her mind as she ran from the house back to the shelter through the deep snow, while packing her only possible solutions…food and covers.

As Grandma again approached the little one, its hind legs had been pulled under it more comfortably and its neck had curled around settling its head onto its shoulders. (Like you can see deer pictured when they are just resting.) The frost-covered eyelashes were closed. *Does that mean it is dead? There is no movement, but it does look more comfortable.* Questions flooded her mind as she approached it, but it never moved. Grandma touched its legs and it still did not move, so she started caressing the body and felt warmth, but not the slightest movement. *Surely, I just followed it into the shelter, so maybe it is still alive.* As she touched the little body, she could feel that there was not much flesh on those bones. It was very tiny and apparently desperately starved. When she touched its head, she felt many small hard bumps and knew those were ticks engorged with blood, the deer's blood.

It had an infestation of ticks which covered its head, lower jaws, and down its neck, some were still crawling, but most were deeply embedded and plump with its blood. Even with all of Grandma's touching, the fawn did not flinch a muscle. If she had not felt the warmth of its body, Grandma would have been certain it was dead. She put applesauce to its mouth, but there was no movement. Anything solid she knew would not be good to put into its mouth so she did not attempt that. That left only the ticks to be dealt with. It would take some kind of powder or spray used on animals but she could not think of anything like that available at the farm.

Desperately she kept hoping for the best, and knew that at the house she could get dog shampoo used to kill fleas. That was the only thing she thought might get rid of ticks without harming the fawn. Anyway, she hoped that would not harm the fawn, but it may have. That seemed her only alternative.

After another rush to the house to get the shampoo, she began with rubber gloves on both hands. She saturated the most infested hair, then grabbed the crawling ticks and pulled out the embedded ones. As she pulled them off the fawn she crushed them angrily against the board wall, even though she knew it was hard to kill a tick. The family way to ensure tick death was to burn them on a hot stove or with a match, but neither way could be done at the shelter.

Finally, she covered the frail little body with pieces of blankets and rags for warmth, then tried again to get food into Orphan's mouth. That failed. There was no reaction, no mouth movements. It could not get any nourishment. *Never put **anything** in the mouth of a patient who is not conscious...deer would be the same,* she recalled. Nothing else she had carried down could be used to feed the fawn. She was too late with food! Really, little else had been in her power but maybe, with strength from food, it could have survived its other challenges.

The best Grandma could hope for was to warm Orphan's little body on this horribly cold night. It was sheltered from the increasing wind and snow, but one side of the shelter was wide open to the cold with no way to cover the large opening. There was not even a light to help them solve this problem *"What to do? What to do? Maybe, find something to hang over the opening...But it's getting too dark to do that."* She mumbled the possibilities and came up with no solution.

Grandpa came down, just as it was becoming dark, to help cover the little deer with a heavy old rug. Before covering, its head was straightened out to rest on the ground so it would not suffocate under the rug. That was a flawed decision--a thoughtful but flawed decision. Its head needed access to air and the tick killer rubbed on its body smelled like ether which the deer should not breathe. Under the rug was ether, but outside the rug was exposure to the freezing temperature. *What to do? What to do?* She did what she had to do. She had to go to the house. In darkness all possibilities had ended. They could not see to do anything more for the little fawn. It was so terribly hard for Grandma to go to the house and leave Orphan alone in that subzero weather, but without electricity in the shelter what else could she do after darkness had settled in?

She went inside and prayed and barely slept, so greatly regretting that she had not put apples--many, many, many, apples on that cement step the day before.

There was also fear "niggling at Grandma's mind." Ticks can be deadly to humans also. Grandpa had been helping cover the little deer and he would continue to help if needed. They both were near enough to the tick infestation to be in danger. Somehow Grandma tried to put that fear for herself and for Grandpa out of her mind, but it still slipped into her thoughts as she struggled to get to sleep. Time did not allow them to do the garment change and shower which is recommended after being in a tick environment. Tomorrow would need to be their chance to fight that possibility.

She did believe the next morning might bring renewed hope. She even hoped that she might find Orphan standing when she got back to him. What a gift that would be from Mother Nature or maybe from Father God.

That was not what she found the next morning. Orphan had not moved, but instead the cold had frozen its face. Eyes, tongue, ears, nose, and mouth were all solid. There was no way the fawn could come out of this because of its frozen body parts. So, Grandma conceded that Mother Nature was going to have to take over completely. It must die because it could not survive with damaged parts, those frozen through the night. Though there was warmth under the rug, there was no future for Orphan. Grandpa took the rug off to let the cold finish its job.

Orphan had many foes against him--mankind, ticks, hunger, cold, and even his own herd. He had lost the battle, though he had tried valiantly to survive. Humans had been one of his foes. In many ways they had helped him lose his battle for survival. Without the mother deer to help her fawn survive this first hard winter, its battle was too tough to fight alone. His life was short and much of it was painful. If Orphan really was Little Buck, then his little "olive nubbins" would never become a "crown with many points."

Grandma would never be sure if Orphan and Little Buck were one and the same, but she had to say good-bye to both on that sad day. Grandpa had to dispose of fawn remains again, much as he had done a few years before with the fawn which had been killed by the cougar behind their barn. This baby was very light and little from starvation, so Grandpa could easily lift it. Grandma appreciated Grandpa. He had to do what he had to do. They both knew that.

Soon, Grandpa had loaded the little body into the pickup and headed toward the hills. Grandma stayed home and cried. She had so many regrets! Was that orphan fawn really the Little Buck? Grandma thought it was. The cat food, stolen from under the door, must have been dug out by those same small hooves which Grandma had seen as a baby playing with Dawna, Little-un, and Big-un. She remembered his little nose and tongue reaching through the wires of the yard fence for bird seed. The little doe, Dawna, also down on her knees, tried the same. Perhaps she was following his lead. Anyway, they both showed the tops of their heads, his with nubbins, hers without. His would never get to hold a majestic crown of antlers.

Grandma's sad thoughts flooded her mind. *How could I not have known? Why didn't I get him food– any kind of food? How could I have let my fear of the dark keep me from finding apples for him? His rumpled hair was a sign of ticks, which had hatched in the warm spell, finding him an easy host. Is it possible a mother deer would have chewed the pests from him? How could I have laughed at his messy hair when he was struggling against such an infestation? I am so sorry for failing this innocent little one who turned to me for help and I was not sensitive enough to know his need. And mostly, God, how can I keep this from ever happening again? Surely, Father God, you can be there, especially for the orphans.*

Those "little black-olive nubbins," once seen on Little Buck's head between his ears, made a permanent sweet memory in Grandma's mind. She would never have seen them if he had not stuck his little fawn nose under the yard fence to eat birdseed.

"A soft, velvety hair covers the antlers until they are full-grown." (This was stated in the Encyclopedia.) Little Buck must have had that "soft, velvety hair" on his budding antlers as a baby, and Grandma felt lucky to have seen that. She learned so very much from watching him from the time he was a baby until she had to say "Good-Bye" to him. But she did not learn enough soon enough. Grandma felt lucky she knew Little Buck in **the best way humans can know a wild animal, with her heart**.

Life flourishes on the Five-Acre Farm.

Chp. 16: "Hope for the Future"

After snow melted away and roads dried enough for Grandma to walk off winter's blues and her weight gain, she donned her tennis shoes and headed down the road between the hill and their farm.

The air was fresh and sweet as she studied the hillside and walked. One white area caught her attention beside a fence on the north/hill side of the road. It had shades of brown and black surrounding it and looked to be about the size of a deer. Grandma's heart sank! *Could this be the remains of a fawn after winter scavengers cleaned the bones to whiteness? Is it possible Little-un was trapped behind a fence while trying to escape a predator? Did her injured foot make her slow and unable to jump?* "Stop imagining!" Grandma scolded herself. "There is nothing to be gained in this kind of thinking. Maybe that is only a pile of rocks." Her eyes left the "pile," but her mind revisited it often.

Another day later in the summer Grandma saw several deer in the barn brush patch when she was packing kitchen scraps to the shed. Before the deer startled and ran away, she saw clearly one was an older doe with a split ear, one was a little yearling doe, and one was a young buck with two points on his right antler and three on his left. The antlers were beautiful but had thin upright prongs, a sign of youth. The young antlers were still coated with heavy gray "velvet," that covering which protects them as they grow again every year from their original "olive-sized nubbins."

This must be our deer family! Grandma's thoughts raced, *…Mother Nature and God's 'plan for the future.' This is interesting…they have Mother Nature and Father God and Grandma and Grandpa. Of course, Grandmas and Grandpas really do not have much control of their families, but there is that element of loving availability which grandparents are known for.*

"Is that you Adolescent? Will you be staying long?" she asked just as the deer "turned tail and sped away" --a deer lesson well learned. They jumped the fence and headed west. "Be wise, little family. Be wise and careful and maybe I'll see you again," Grandma said a fond temporary farewell while Miss Kitty followed her to the barn. Miss Kitty knew there would be kitchen scraps for her when they reached the shed. Miss Kitty seemed to like her human friends…at least she liked their food.

Fuzzy Butt no longer had the strength to go to the barn nor the will to leave the yard, even though at one time this had been a big adventure for him. Miss Kitty, now fully grown and very strong-willed, had filled his job of entertaining their humans. Though she was a female, she never had kittens--a fact that led to the conclusion she must have been spayed in her earlier home.

Miss Kitty often demanded Fuzzy Butt's attention. When he was younger, she would taunt him into a chase which she always won. In these older years, when he barked at her, sometimes it might even cause him to land on his weak little behind. Life had gotten very difficult for him, and Miss Kitty did not understand that. He no longer could hear and his vision was getting poor. After all, he was seventeen years old. For humans that would have been 119 years old, using the 7 people years to 1 dog year ratio.

There was one night when Fuzzy Butt was out "for business" and Miss Kitty ran a challenge past him. When he would not chase her, she charged at him from behind, stopping just short of a collision. That did not get his attention, so she circled the big tree which he was sniffing and popped out in front of his face, but he still did not react.

"What's the matter Little White Dog? Don't you see me?" Miss Kitty seemed to say as she gave up her effort to play and haughtily walked away.

Trapper, aka Fuzzy Butt, got much more fragile. He seemed to sleep most of the time, but when not sleeping he walked circles, as if mentally confused. His little back was humped and his tail no longer stood upright in a curl. He was in pain. There was no joy in his life.

The old Mitchell couple struggled with thoughts of permanently ending his pain. That was a hard decision, but it was finally made. He did not know he had so completely-filled human lives with love-- both giving and receiving love. This final decision was very hard for them because of that love for their pet. It was with pain, but it was time to say "Good-bye, our sweet little friend."

He did not know he was helped on that trip away, because he had become comatose and did not know the veterinarian was making his sleep final. Grandma and Grandpa cried! They cried a lot! Nights were even sleepless requiring midnight drives just to dim their pain. Animals can mean that much to humans.

One morning, after the story of "Orphan" was started, an idea "landed in Grandma's mind," as so often happens when awakening and still in a drowsy state. *There is scripture about the deer. "As the deer panteth for the water...." Yessss! God included deer in His Holy Book!* Then she drowsily contemplated, *...But how can I get apples to feed the hungry?*

In the fall Grandma had collected apples from neighborhood orchards and even from beside the road where deer were sometimes standing in danger just to eat fallen apples. But winter had diminished her supply, leaving her with a problem.

The preceding night she had put apple cores and peelings on the cement steps. The following morning all apple parts had disappeared, so she knew there again had been night deer visitors. But the stored apples in their cellar had rotted. Now she had nothing to feed the hungry.

One later night, before she had gone to bed, she saw a tiny White Tail baby wandering in the half-light of the receding Blue Moon. The baby was seen as a dark silhouette against the moonlit meadow. Its large tail was hanging down, and clearly showed long thick whiteness, as it walked away. Grandma's heart had raced...*Not another Orphan! It's so tiny and all alone ... or maybe that was just a coyote?*

Grandma then used her high-powered flashlight to see, but by then the silhouette had moved into the corral and out of sight. However, there in the "Garden of Eden" were other deer. They must have been other White Tails attracted by hay which Grandpa had put there. Some were standing with their heads down, and some had alert ears and bright shiny eyes looking toward the flashlight. "Good! The little one has a family." Grandma whispered in the darkness of her house. She was relieved another fawn was not in a mortal struggle, at least not one she knew about.

After that, the White Tails often visited the farm and grazed on the hillside beyond. One doe had tiny twin fawns; they were tiny because that is the way it is with delicate-shaped White Tails. Their color seemed lighter and even racks on the bucks would have a different lean to them. Of course, their tails told the final tale, being white, fuller, and longer.

A few mellow springtime mornings later, and after the recent deer visits, Grandma sat on an upside-down bucket beside a little grave. The grave was newly made and marked with a homemade cement stone placed in the garden beneath the petite prune tree where their pet rested. She was nearly crazy with grief, as the gentle crisp breeze kissed her cheeks and tickled through her hair. Subtle tears flowed, gentle persistent tears. Fuzzy Butt's age had made life intolerable for him. It seemed the most merciful thing to do was to give him peace, even though his death would bring the old couple pain.

After he was gone, loneliness, doubts, and the most horrible heartache came for Grandma and Grandpa from his absence. Many times, long after midnight, they even drove to the distant town the distant town, just because they could not sleep. Fuzzy Butt had filled their lives with happiness, so they felt strong emotional pain after their loss. Loss of an animal can be that painful!

"Oh, Fuzzy Butt, our sweet pet, we loved you so, … and we always will." Grandma patted the fresh dirt surface as if the sweet little friend beneath it would know her heart's grief. Fuzzy Butt had been a much greater part of Grandma and Grandpa's adult lives than anything else, except their children. He was like family, and they had loved him as such. "Thank you, God, for giving him to us for nearly seventeen years. Thank you, little white four-legged friend, for forcing me outside during nighttime darkness, though the nights were often fear-filled. Because of you, I experienced nature at night. And thank you Fuzzy Butt, our sweet little friend, for loving us."

Grandma clutched her Bible to her chest seeking comfort, peace, and knowledge that God cares for "All His Creatures." Sometimes, the pain in Grandma's heart literally felt like a physical shattering, but even so, life goes on and Grandpa needed her to be strong for him. He, likewise, suffered but tried to be strong for her, though there were times when he also shed hidden tears. Men do not like to admit it, but they love deeply, too.

Grandma and Grandpa spent many sleepless nights missing their little white friend. It was good they could console each other and even get into the car and travel to distant places, unplanned but distracting places, to keep their minds off their loss. Even a short drive helped. Also, sunny days helped take away their gloom and this one bright spring morning felt like peace.

While sitting beside the little grave, Grandma asked for God's comfort and it came. A single wistful, **"Churk,"** from a turkey followed the morning breeze to her ears. A single distant, **"Honk,"** from a goose permeated the damp mist of morning, and then she heard many calls from the flight of geese moving from the river to graze in a nearby field. Nature's sounds caressed her like a soft blanket, easing and comforting her heart. The sun warmed the house and buildings around it, and peaceful silence from the grave seemed to tell her, "He is sleeping…be at peace." Her hand had to pat the dirt as if saying, "Good night, little one."

A soothing internal comfort, the comfort of the Five-Acre Farm blessed with nature's creatures and God in control, carried Grandma from the calming moment. She went quietly inside to be with Grandpa while thinking deeply. *Why is life so short? Why must there be death? How can loss of what is loved so much be accepted?* Grandma knew she had no answers for these questions, but she was grateful for the presence of Earth's many wonderful creatures which strengthen and comfort us through life's trials.

Spring on the Five-Acre Farm came as it regularly does throughout the valley. When spring came, Mother Nature started replenishing the cycle of life. Flowers pushed tendrils up through moist soil, and grassy meadows became a green carpet. Babies of all sorts appeared. Wild flower scents wafted from blossoms on bushes, trees, and plants on the ground. Prolific green buds sprouted to feed hungry animals when bushes and trees again came to life. Winter wildlife no longer struggled to find food, then bodies shrunken from hunger again became healthy. The Earth smiled!

The birth bushes in the little bottom field would begin to dry up. Then the crushed grasses and weeds would serve as a comfortable mat to welcome the birth of one or more baby deer. Probably in beginning of June Grandma would start watching for frequent visits by does, because that was a clue about future happenings. It seemed, perhaps after a doe's birth there, in this later year, that would be repeated by bringing forth new babies.

Baby bunnies somewhere were probably just learning to hop, so they could race and jump and make mischief very soon. *Will they come to celebrate Easter?* With a smile Grandma thought, *Ha, old woman you are being silly.*

The little hen turkey might return to her hidden nest on the adjoining five acres to raise another family for this summer. It had worked well in the years past for her. Food, water, and seclusion were all she needed. She could do the rest.

Baby Robins might chirp urging their parents to hurry, **"Feed me! Feed me! Feed me, here!"** And Mama Robin would have a family to love again, a purpose for her life.

Will Dovey and Al return? Maybe.

"Wild turkey poults are able to fly in about three to four weeks, but stay with their mother until they are about four months old."

(Quote from National Wild Turkey Federation, NWTF)
(Photo by Joe Foster @ NWTF.net)
(Contact NWTF by MStewart @ NWTF.)

Chp. 17: "Alpenglow"

When age made the older couple more fragile, life on the Five-Acre Farm became very difficult, but Grandma will forever have sweet memories made there. Circumstances took the Mitchells away from the farm, but one special memory will bless her life forever, a picture painted on her mind that encompassed God's wonderful world in just one scene.

It happened this way. The evening meal was over and she and Grandpa were settling into their evening routines. He usually sat in front of the TV, while Grandma did whatever her heart desired. This night she chose to walk.

There was still snow on the ground so, as the sun dimmed, the air started to cool. Her jacket was beginning to allow cold to seep through, even though her arms snugged around her middle. Cold would not send her away from this escape from the mundane to the privacy of Earth's natural beauty.

Yes, Grandma had melancholy moments drifting through her mind as she walked. She knew the rich sweetness of this place near the mountains had molded Grandpa and herself into different people, better people. There had been other "nature walks" when Grandpa accompanied her but those were special talking times, not memory walks. Both kinds were good, but this one time was very special.

This evening walk gave Grandma a chance to just remember the good parts of her life. As she looked across the valley she saw homes, farmed fields, roads, and many signs of humans residing not far from the Five-Acre Farm. She could envision the school bus and many log trucks which had traveled the very road she was walking. That road at first was just a dusty gravel route, then it was covered with black asphalt with even a yellow painted mid-line. The dust in those first years blew south in the summer and north in the winter. Wind then brought either road dust or winter blizzards, but there were many more sunny days to enjoy the fresh country air.

The sweetest of her memories, of course, were their two children born three years apart. They had been raised on the farm. The boy and girl had grown up knowing and loving animals. They had played and romped, built forts, jumped rope, rode horses, picked fruit, built tree houses, tented in the yard, entertained friends, crashed a scooter, learned to ride a motorcycle, loved many pets, even learned to drive a car while making circles around the field in the lowest gear Grandpa could set for the car. Green "Poppin Johnny" gave their son the feeling of being a caterpillar driver from the time he was very young.

Grandma smiled inside, a sweetness that cannot be contained when remembering her children and the many memories which filled her life. She could almost hear their voices, a girl's giggles and a husky boy's laugh. They were such good children, grown into excellent adults.

The children grew well and healthy and moved on to make good lives with good spouses. Then they even brought more little ones into the family. Their educations were all completed with degrees. However, that meant the jobs to follow would take them away from the farm. How could a parent, or grandparent, wish anything else? But it left a lonely spot in Grandma and Grandpa's lives.

Pets, "from ponies to pigs, and more," had been a part of the farm's residents. Wild animal visitors, "mostly four-legged and winged," spiced the days, months, and years. Grandma did very little gardening for lack of skill, but also because of her willingness to consider their crops as wild animal feed. She refused to claim soil for personal benefit if it was needed by animals.

Cattle did graze the small fields, but a greater joy was to see the deer grazing on new tender grass. Mostly the cattle were fed there so dry crops would not be there to fuel a wildfire. No monetary gain was made from cattle grazing, and it did not take long for the grass of the fields to be shortened and protected from fire. They were small fields, divided for convenience. The bottom portion was mostly saved for wildlife and therefore became the "birth bushes" for deer babies, or bird families.

When Grandma topped the rise in the road, she stopped to look across the hills and the valley. It was then she experienced the awesome "scene." Bright colors surrounded her! She felt wrapped in it. It almost felt heavy because the colors were so strong.

The sinking sun had set fire to the sky with a blaze that reflected on puffy clouds which drifted beneath an umbrella of blue, yet even then grayness crowded in on the far side of the valley. Their world was wrapped in a beautiful sunset, horizon to horizon. Blues, pinks, and oranges were so brilliant they could almost be inhaled. While stopping and absorbing every aspect of the beauty, she saw hills blazing with pink, pink cotton-candy clouds, a small pond toward town was mirroring the blue skies above complete with those pink clouds showing on the water, white snowdrifts in low spots were also turned pink by the sunset's radiance, a brilliant blaze of color-on-color was reflecting on the buildings at their farm as she looked downward toward home.

This evening sunset show has been called Alpenglow (Webster says the word comes "from *Alpengluhen"* referring to brightly colored sunrise or sunset shining on the mountains of Germany.) and truly the valley's mountains did glow with color. Where they were white with snow, that had become the softest pink. Mt Harris was as pink as a lollipop and even seemed to shine.

Then she saw the big window at the end of the farm's house, behind which Grandpa often sat to watch TV or watch various other animals at the birdseed feeder and near the barn. Perhaps he was even there in that chair at that exquisite moment.

To top it off, the scene held a young deer, maybe a fawn, standing motionless outside the yard. Maybe it was at the birdseed but possibly looking into that window. (Her mind places the fawn looking directly at the big window, but maybe it was not. Her mind does remember the little deer was standing there a long time, as if looking into that window.)

The little deer would not have been the one called "Orphan" because at that time he was gone forever. There was another little set of orphaned fawns, which had later found the Five-Acre Farm as a haven. Grandma called the twins Sis and Brudda (Brother). Their mother was found dead beside the road.

Grandma only assumed that was the fawns' mother because their arrival at the farm was shortly after the doe's body was seen. She appeared to have been killed by a car and her body remained damaged off to the right just beyond the nearby road corner. Regardless, two little fawns found the Five-Acre Farm as a place of safety. Sis stayed for a while, but Brudda returned to the herd. It just may be that the fawn at the window during the beautiful sunset was Sis or Brudda. ("Sis" has quite a story to tell about survival. Her story may become part of another book called "Haven.")

Grandma did not want to disturb the little deer by walking home soon, so she just stood and absorbed the scene until the colors started to fade. Slowly, it seemed a curtain fell closing the day, leading to darkness. There were still colors, but now more purples and greys, hinting at shadows.

Grandma knew she must walk quickly to get home before complete darkness. It would be dangerous to be walking in the dark where vehicles might be traveling rapidly up the road. So with hesitation, she left while holding inside her mind the beauty of that show which nature had just displayed. When she got closer to their Five-Acre Farm she discovered the little fawn had left, but she did not see it leave.

Love for all the wonders in this wonder-filled world, including Grandpa and that little deer, emblazoned the scene forever in Grandma's mind, as she walked back to their house on the Five-Acre Farm and all that she loved. The farm had held so very many sweet memories of their children, their parents, other family members, their friends, their many years making it a home, and the many precious animals which had joined them on this journey called "life."

Grandma and Grandpa saw much of nature and learned to love the earth and its animals. The older couple were richly blessed by having their home which sat between the mountains and the town. There they saw many animal hardships and struggles, which in some ways resembled human experiences. They also saw animal emotions: joy, love, grief, need, selfishness, fear, and many more human-like emotions. They saw the animals in a special way, "with their hearts, as well as with their eyes."

Human eyes see material things, but their hearts see real things.

The Alpenglow Sunset

(The above picture perfectly fits Grandma's experience before leaving the farm. That is the road on which she walked and this was a real sunset. This picture was taken by Grandma.)

This author believes strongly that humans have a responsibility to take good care of wildlife, especially those animals which are herbivores. Humans are their protectors—their only protectors. Humans and carnivores can be enemies of wild creatures, but humans can be compassionate and take actions which make life easier for the Earth's wildlife. Baby animals of all kinds especially need wise human policies to provide them good lives.

Since this author experienced wildlife in a rural part of Oregon, she is especially aware of the difficulties experienced by young deer (fawns) and young elk (calves). She has some suggestions which might make life easier for them. Here these suggestions will be called "Maybes."

- Maybe fences could have their bottom wires raised more than a foot above the ground. They need to be high enough to allow baby animals to crawl underneath rather than get trapped by fence wires when crawling between the wires or jumping over them. [See page 19, paragraphs #5, #6; pages 68 and 69 for information about difficulties of fences.]

- Maybe any season that allows the killing of doe deer or cow elk could be stopped, since it is very hard for a hunter to determine if a doe or cow is "dry." ("Dry means she has no baby… can result in a slow and painful death for her baby.") [See page 31, paragraphs #4, and #5 for information.]

- Maybe traps should only be put in a location where deer or elk feet cannot be damaged. Maybe the trap could be placed in an open-sided device, in a root-hole, or under a fallen log. [See pg. 69, paragraphs #2, #3, for an example of the possible damage to deer, elk, or any animal which is not the desired prey.]

- Maybe we should be making more reductions of predatory animals. Currently predators seem to be an increased population while their prey seems to be diminishing. Wolves, cougars, and bear are voracious predators. [See pg. 45, paragraph #6, and pg. 9, all paragraphs.]

- Maybe we should not kill those noisy Magpies. They eat from the backs of living animals… ticks, etc. Ticks are a threat to most living mammals. (This author has seen a Magpie with that purpose on the back of a resting deer.) [See pg. 85, paragraph #6.]

- Maybe humans should be saving poor quality fruit for winter feed for hungry wildlife of many kinds. [See page 90, paragraphs #8 and #9; page 11, paragraph #5 and #6. See pg. 82, paragraph #3 through #8

- Maybe, since elk are fed through hard winters, it would be a good policy to also provide "deer feeding stations." There are pellets palatable to deer but hay, such as that fed to elk, may not be good for them. [See pg. 81, paragraph #3 and #5.]

<>&<>&<>~~~~~ **Author Information** ~~~~~~~<>&<>&<>

The author of this book is also the character called Grandma. Her spouse really is the character called Grandpa, but he preferred to have a diminutive role in the story, though not so in her life. She has written the story as exactly as she recalls it. Of course, the words of human conversations may not be exact, but the concepts remain true.

The author, whose pseudonym is Lynn Ernestine, believes this book to be of the genre called "Creative Nonfiction." Her story gives animal actions as she saw them but she makes italicized "word thoughts" for those animals like their actions would imply. "Auditory input" makes a more interesting story to read, therefore this author uses auditory/thought creativity. She believes that, if the animal could talk, the boldface print words might be the ones they would say.

The pictures are mostly as she photographed them. Therefore, she holds the rights to them but willingly shares them in this book to add to its value. Pictures help the words tell the whole story.

Having been raised on a farm, the author lived around a variety of animals and learned about them from her parents whose livelihood was in raising animals. The first five years of her life were spent on a rural homestead where wildlife was also an important part of her family's environment. It is natural that animals would become a significant part of her adult world. She studied them and loved or feared them.

As an adult, she left the farm and attended college to become an elementary teacher. With her Bachelor's Degree she taught for thirty years before retirement. Her teaching was at a variety of grade levels and to different ability levels.

Marriage to "Grandpa" was at age twenty-two and two children blessed their lives. The couple recently celebrated their Sixtieth Wedding Anniversary and they really are a "Grandma and Grandpa."

Though animals have been a part of the author's whole life, her understanding of them became even greater during those years while living at the Five-Acre Farm. There she studied animals closely to the point of emotional connection. **She deeply felt what she wrote and wrote only what she truly saw.**

This book is written with a purpose. It is intended to influence those readers with the power to affect life or death for animals, by demonstrating the suffering human decisions can make. Especially significant is the decision to separate baby animals from their parents. Nature needs to be allowed to decide when babies can survive without their parent. Killing animal mothers inflicts terrible misery on their babies and often brings death, as this story demonstrates. The author hopes the information shared within will bring more compassion into our culture.

Other books by this author:

- "There's a Dinosaur on My Chair" (Picture Book)
- "Tiny Turkey Terrorized Tutorville" (Lower through middle grades,) Illustrated, Alliteration
- "Widdie, Pibbles, and the Purple Powder" (Lower grades.) Illlustrated, Chapter Book.
- "Foods of the Promised Land" (Adult) Homestead History of NE Oregon
- "God Working Wonders" (Adult) "Right Writers" Personal Anecdotes
- "Grandma's Doodles" (Adult) Coloring Book.
- "Kuntree Kuzzins" (Adult) Cartoon Collection
- "The Truth Is in The Heart, A Fact-Based Theory of the Jenny Wiley Story" (Adult) See online browser to learn about Jenny Wiley.
- "Through the Grain" (Middle grades,) Chapter Book, Handicapped, and mixed-race characters.

If interested in any of these books call 541-962-0299
or email gordoncreekacres@gmail.com

The author, Lynn Ernestine